THE NANDI OF KENYA

THE
NANDI
OF
KENYA

*LIFE CRISIS RITUALS IN
A PERIOD OF CHANGE*

BY

MYRTLE S. LANGLEY

FOREWORD BY F. B. WELBOURN

ST. MARTIN'S PRESS · NEW YORK

ISBN 0-312-55884-8

Library of Congress Cataloging in Publication Data

Langley, Myrtle.
    The Nandi of Kenya.

    Abridgement of the author's thesis, University of
Bristol, 1976.
        Bibliography: p.
        1. Nandi (African tribe) — Rites and ceremonies.
I. Title.
DT433.542.L372   1979   392'.09676'2   78-31186
ISBN 0-312-55884-8

To the memory of my parents
and for Africa

Printed in Great Britain

Acknowledgements

The work which follows is an abridgement of my doctoral dissertation submitted to the University of Bristol in 1976. It was my privilege to be supervised by the Rev. F.B. Welbourn and I wish to express my special thanks to him for his enthusiasm, help and friendship — they proved a constant encouragement. My thanks also go to Drs Donald R. Jacobs and Okot p'Bitek for their kind supervision while I was a Research Associate at the Institute of African Studies in the University of Nairobi.

No opportunity, however, of engaging in this fascinating piece of research would have been afforded me apart from the Nandi and their missionaries. To all my friends among the people and in the missions I record my sincerest thanks.

It proved necessary to collect numerous records and read through quantities of material, and in this respect I should like to thank the following: the Chief Archivist and staff of the Kenya National Archives; the Registrar General, Nairobi; the Librarians and staffs of the Bristol University Library, the Macmillan Library at Nairobi, Makerere University Library at Kampala, Pitt-Rivers Museum at Oxford, and the School of Oriental and African Studies at the University of London; the staffs at Eldoret Hospital, Kapsabet Court, Kapsabet District Offices, Kapsabet Hospital and Nandi Hills Dispensary; the mission staffs at the Africa Inland Church at Kapsabet, the Anglican Church at Kapsabet, the Catholic Mission at Chepterit, Kobujoi, Kaiboi and Tindinyo, the Full Gospel Church at Chemelil and Nandi Hills, the International Pentecostal Assemblies Mission at Chepkumia, the Pentecostal Assemblies of Canada Mission at Nyang'ori, the Reformed Church of East Africa at Eldoret and the Seventh-day Adventist Church at Kaigat.

Acknowledgement is made to the Oxford University Press for kind permission to reproduce 3 Plates from *The Nandi* by A.C. Hollis (Plates 1, 4 and 8 in the present work).

I must also express my sincere gratitude to all those who extended to me hospitality and friendship during my periods of residence in Nandi, and to colleagues and friends who helped in different ways with the production of a final manuscript.

Bristol, July 1978   Myrtle S. Langley

v

Contents

Contents

Plates

Figures

Maps

Foreword

Ever since van Gennep introduced the concept in 1908, 'rites of passage' have been integral to both anthropological and religious studies. Whenever a change in status takes place, it is accompanied by ritual; and this is true whether in the relatively sophisticated rituals of marriage or graduation in the West or in the (to western eyes) exotic rites of circumcision and clitoridectomy in many African societies. It is true also whether the rites are still seen as integral to the process of social maturation or increasingly regarded as 'mere ritual'. The importance of their study in an African society is not simply their scholarly interest but the insights which can be gained into the dynamics of that society and the clues which they provide for an understanding of the West. Dr Langley has chosen to study three life crises among the Nandi of East Africa — initiation into adulthood, marriage and divorce; and perhaps her most important contribution is her study of female initiation. Only a woman could do this; and Dr Langley has added a significant chapter to the work in this field already published by Monica Wilson and Audrey Richards. But equally fully — and with a deep empathy for the Nandi — she has treated the other facets of her survey. She came to Nandi at a time when traditional rituals — already for many years under attack by Christian missionaries — were suffering the much more radical influences of secularisation and nationalism. She has therefore been able to present not only the oral and archival evidence of the rites as they were but a contemporary study of the rites as they are developing under extra-tribal forces. There are still those Nandi for whom the traditional rites — however unwittingly changed by the coming of Europeans — are integral to a proper manhood and a proper womanhood. At the other end of the spectrum are those who regard them with as deep scepticism as their fellows in the West. In between are many varieties of attitude struggling to discover — and expressing their struggle in changing symbols — how it is possible to be at the same time both Nandi and Kenyan and to grasp the benefits of a technological world view. The changing symbols Dr Langley describes and interprets at length; and there emerges a picture of a deeply uncertain society struggling to discover a new self-image which shall be faithful both to the Nandi past and to the new values of the post-colonial age. In this it is by no means dissimilar from the uncertain western society which can produce such movements as motor cycle cults and hippies described by Paul Willis in his *Profane Culture* (Routledge and Kegan Paul, 1978). It is through an exploration of changing symbolisms that Africa and the West can contribute both to their own self-understanding and to their understanding of each other.

Bristol University   F.B. Welbourn

I. Asking Questions

It was during the years 1966-8 that I first came to know the Nandi.[1] By then, almost half a century had elapsed since the final and abortive Nandi attempt actively to resist British rule, and the changes initiated by trader, colonial administrator, missionary and educator were well set in. Moreover, only three years previously, independence had come to the nation of Kenya and a new national consciousness was beginning to percolate through to local level. It was during this initial stay that my interest was first aroused in the subject of life crisis rituals.

At dawn and dusk, in season, sounds of tinkling bells and shrill whistles wafted through the still air from the fields to the rear of my house. By day girls, dressed in long leather skirts with heads hooded, walked warily, if at all, in groups along the nearby lanes. In the course of daily work missionary colleagues bemoaned the fact that promising young students, male and female, were being forced to go through 'customs'. 'Why the bells, whistles and hoods?' I asked. Whence the 'customs'? What of the antagonism?

Persistently, at tutorials, I listened to male students lamenting their lot in life. How, with the exploitation of the time-honoured custom of bridewealth, could they ever hope to marry? Surely parents were putting an insuperable obstacle in their way when they demanded vast sums of money and large numbers of cattle for their educated daughters?

Hard and fast, in the course of church deliberations, came the rhetorical questions: 'Why do elders of the church take second wives, thus "reverting" to polygamy?' 'Why do so many unmarried girls become pregnant? This used not to be in Nandi.'

Repeatedly, in the course of daily living, I encountered unfamiliar customs. For example, one evening, as I took a stroll through the fields with a friend, we were stopped and greeted by an old woman. 'Is it well?' she enquired. 'Is it well, old woman?' we responded. 'Are you well?' she continued. 'Yes' we replied. Whereupon she proceeded in the usual Nandi manner to enquire after husband, children and livestock. Perplexity and bewilderment, however, followed the disclosure that neither of us had a husband either in Kenya or overseas. Nevertheless she went on, undaunted, to enquire after the children. But no children! This was indeed impossible, unbelievable! Yet, she had to concede eventually, true. We then parted on the understanding that she would make appropriate and discreet arrangements for the begetting of children, husband or no! Only later did I realise the full implications of her kind-hearted promise: she was alluding to the practice of 'woman marriage' and the custom of engaging the services of a visiting genitor.

Subsequently, archival research and field work in 1973 preceded

1

and followed by intensive reading were to enable me to answer many of these questions, but not without prior knowledge of the Nandi people, their culture and their history.

NOTES

1 I was tutor in religious education at Mosoriot Teachers College, situated between Kapsabet and Eldoret, from 1966-8.

II. The Nandi

1. *People and District*

The Nandi are an East African people. They belong to the so-called Kalenjin cluster which, together with the Dadog (Tatoga), descends from the 'Highland' Nilotes — one of three main branches of a parent Nilotic people. The parent group has been successively classified by ethnographers as 'Nilo-Hamites', 'Paranilotes' and most recently 'Highland', 'Plains' and 'River-Lake' Nilotes.[1]

The 'Highland' Nilotes are believed to have been centred in the highlands of western Kenya, from the south-eastern shores of Lake Victoria eastward through the Rift Valley and southward into Tanzania, since about A.D. 1,000.

The Kalenjin divide further, for purposes of classification, into four sub-groups: (1) the Pokot (Suk) and Marakwet of the Rift Valley; (2) the Sabaot (including the Kony) of Mount Elgon; (3) the Keiyo and Tugen (Kamasia) on the floor and sides of the Rift Valley; and (4) the Kipsigis (mis-named Lumbwa), Terik (or Nyang'ori) and Nandi (Chemng'al). None of these sub-groups is in itself homogeneous. For example, the Marakwet may be divided into six principal political groups and the Sabaot into four. Yet all share a common cultural and linguistic heritage.

The name 'Nandi' was first mentioned in writing by Johann Ludwig Krapf in 1854 and first put on the map by H.M. Stanley in 1878.[2] Derived from a Swahili word *mnandi*, meaning 'cormorant' and presumably signifying 'voraciousness', it was used by traders, missionaries and colonial authorities to refer to the Kalenjin generally and more particularly to the sub-group known both to themselves and others as the *Chemng'al*.[3] The name 'Kalenjin' is of more recent origin. Derived from a Kipsigis word meaning 'I tell [told] you' it was coined deliberately by an educated African élite to underline the common heritage of traditions, culture and language linking the separate Kalenjin entities.[4]

Today the Nandi inhabit Nandi District and its surrounding areas in the highlands of western Kenya. The District lies on a plateau which extends from the Mau mountain range on the east and south-east to the Nyanza Plains on the west and from the Sosiani River in the north to the Kano Plains in the south. The southern and western limits of the Nandi plateau are well defined by granite escarpments rising steeply from the plains. Its average elevation is 6,000 feet and easy access is available only from the extreme south-west, in which region hills are dotted throughout. The northern region is open grassland with occasional patches of forest in the west and central areas but with hardly any trees on the eastern plains and swamplands. The vegetation

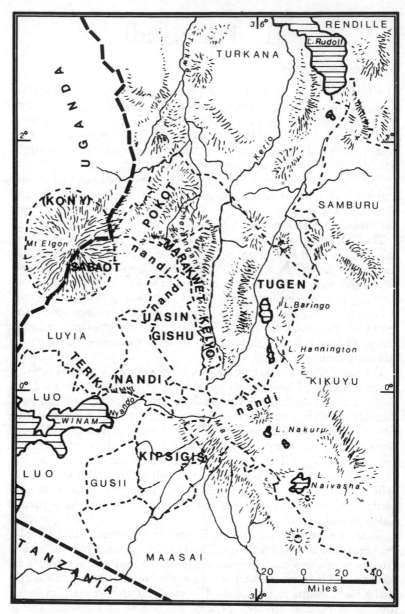

The Kalenjin peoples and their neighbours

of the southern region varies from dense forest, thorn-tree thickets, secondary bush and grass parkland to the sparsely covered hillsides on the edge of the southern escarpment. Below the escarpments the trees are more scattered and stunted and the ground more sparsely covered with the less nutritive grasses.

Numerically, the Nandi are second only to the Kipsigis among the Kalenjin sub-groups. In the 1969 census they totalled 261,969 with 155,543 in Nandi District, 13,589 and 62,551 in the neighbouring districts of Trans Nzoia and Uashin Gishu respectively, and the remainder scattered in various parts of the country. In physique most Nandi are of medium height and of slight build. In movement they are agile and athletic — the Olympic gold medallist Kipchoge Keino is a Nandi. In character and temperament they are honest, frank and ready to acknowledge mistakes, yet proud and independent of spirit, inclined to conservatism and resistant to change. In demeanour they are quiet and undemonstrative, traits which to the outsider can cloak their capacity for deep affection and dogged endurance. In relationships they are generous and hospitable, capable of deep respect and enduring friendship.

2. *Economy and Division of Labour*

Economically, like all Nilotic peoples in the past, the Nandi were pastoralists, cattle being their main interest, but sheep and goats also making their contribution. Today the Nandi economy may be described as pastoral with agriculture. The life of the people is still, however, largely centred in their cattle which remain a major form of wealth. Consequently cattle and related objects have strong ritual value. Not only is the cow in a sense 'sacred' but milk, dung and grass — items connected with the cow — are also 'sacred' and the status of milk is such that its use may be surrounded by a number of taboos.[5] In the past, in particular, division of labour was strict among the Nandi. From the time he was a young child every Nandi was taught to know his proper role by means of a comprehensive educational system which operated in the homes and in the wider community. On the whole, the women cultivated the land and performed all domestic duties while the men herded cattle and went to war. Today the sexes increasingly play an equal part, a large share of the herding being done by the children. Both men and women milk cows, herd cattle, plant, weed and reap crops. Men clear the ground of bush and stumps, cut trees, work iron and make wooden objects, while they also take the cattle to the salt licks. Women, besides looking after the children, prepare food, fetch water and firewood, wash milk vessels, clean the huts and cattle pens, cut grass, and make clothes and pottery. Specialist occupations include, apart from the full-time occupations of iron-working (now rarely undertaken) and

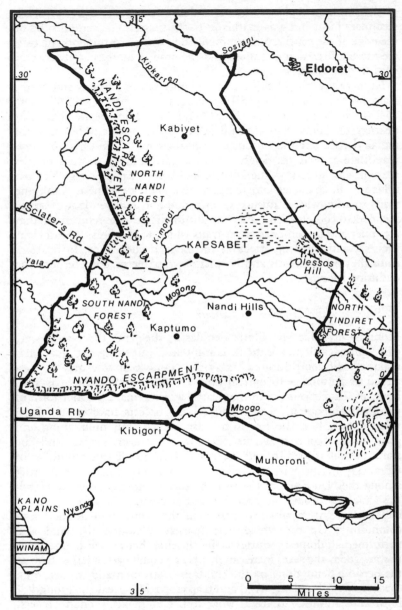

Nandi District showing main physical features
Sclater's Road and the Uganda Railway

pot-making, part-time occupations such as divination, rain-making, tooth-extraction, piercing ear lobes, circumcising and cow-doctoring. Many of the latter are, however, being superseded by professional practitioners in the towns.

3. *Social and Political Organisation*

Socially and politically, the Nandi are organised into households, neighbourhoods and locations. The basic unit of society is the family — the husband with one wife or more and the children. Each wife presides over her own household, the husband spending time with each in turn. About 30 per cent of marriages are polygamous: under modern conditions a second or third wife may manage a second farm or serve in a shop either in town or at the local trading centre. In Nandi there are no villages, but rather households scattered throughout the countryside. The next unit of society, therefore, after the household is the 'neighbourhood' or 'parish' presided over by a council of elders. [6] In the past, neighbourhoods were linked together to form fifteen large areas while these areas were in turn grouped into five large geographical districts. The latter were divided by the British into twenty-five locations administered by headmen through judicial courts. After a sequence of changes these twenty-five became nine locations administered by chiefs and sub-chiefs under a District Commissioner, while the judicial courts were replaced by tribunals. It is important to note that there were no 'chiefs' in Nandi until they were created by the British for administrative convenience. Government was decentralised, power lying with the neighbourhood elders who were represented at higher levels. Only the Nandi ritual expert, known as the *Laibon* and imported from the neighbouring Maasai, exercised any overall control. [7] He was appointed paramount chief by the British in 1906, but until that time he was no more than chief ritual expert in which capacity he was consulted at such times as the seasons for circumcision and planting, the occasions of raiding expeditions and war, and in the event of drought or crisis.

The Nandi have gone down in history for their opposition to British colonial rule. [8] An oft-repeated instance of resistance is their dismantling of the Uganda Railway to replenish their store of arms and their appropriation of the telegraph wires to make ornaments for their women. Between 1896 and 1905-6 the colonial government sent no less than five punitive expeditions against the Nandi. During the last of these their *Laibon*, Koitalel, was killed by a British field officer and the Nandi were placed within a reserve.

There are two other Nandi social groupings, neither of which is localised: the clan and the kindred group. [9] Each clan has a totem or totems. There are seventeen clans and they are exogamous with the exception of those having more than one totem. Marriage is also

forbidden between certain clans. Clan membership is determined
patrilineally. Members of every clan are found throughout Nandi and
in fact many of the younger generation often forget to which clan they
belong. Kinship for a Nandi is a matter of relationship within the
kindred group which consists of cognates and affines whom he calls by
relationship terms stratified according to generations. No Nandi may
marry a member of his own kindred group.

Life is punctuated by a series of *rites de passage*, from the naming
ceremonies connected with birth, through initiation, marriage,
divorce (when necessary), and entrance to adulthood, to the final
funeral ritual. The most important single event of life is initiation,
when a Nandi passes from childhood to adulthood. For the girl it
marks her readiness and preparedness for marriage, for the boy his
training for and entrance into warriorhood. While Nandi no longer
become warriors in the traditional sense, initiation continues to
function in perpetuating the age-set system which in the past was
essential to the social and military organisation of the people. It cuts
across all other distinctions, both the kinship structures of the clan and
the territorial divisions of the neighbourhood areas. At some stage
between the ages of fifteen and twenty-five every Nandi boy was circumcised and admitted to a named age-set, *ibinda*. There were seven
such sets: *Kimnyige, Nyongi, Maina, Chuma, Sawe, Kipkoimet* and
Kaplelach. Every set progressed to a new age-grade approximately
every fifteen years after a 'handing over' ceremony. During his lifetime a man passed through seven age-grades, at least theoretically; in
practice the real distinction lay between three: boys, warriors, and
elders. The length of the recurring cycle was about 105 years.

4. Religion

In Nandi District today, about 100,000 people call themselves
Christians. Of these, half claim membership of the Roman Catholic,
Anglican, Africa Inland and Pentecostal Churches and half claim
adherence to the same or to some small Protestant denomination. Of
the remainder a tiny minority is Muslim and the rest are traditionalists.

The first real contact between the Nandi and Muslims took place
shortly before the middle of the nineteenth century when Arab
caravans began passing through Nandi country to Buganda and east-
wards from the region of the lakes to Maasailand. Prior to this time the
Arabs had failed to arrive at any satisfactory accommodation with the
Nandi concerning either trading transactions or caravan routes
through Nandi territory. For a time all went well until, it is said, the
Arabs humiliated the Nandi and the Nandi retaliated by scaling an
Arab trading post whence only one inmate escaped to tell the tale. The
next major contact between the two peoples did little to improve

matters. The British employed Sudanese soldiers in the punitive expeditions of 1895-1905 and as a result the Nandi developed an antagonism to Muslims generally. In Nandi eyes to be a Muslim was to be 'Arab' or 'Sudanese'. However, when after the Nandi defeat of 1905 Nandi soldiers began to join the army and Nandi men went to work in the towns and on the farms they had to live alongside Muslims, on equal terms. In addition, Sudanese soldiers settled in Nandi as did 'colonies' of Swahili, Somali and other Muslim peoples who were accorded trading rights. Two of these groups, those of Asian and Somali origin, kept more or less to themselves, neither proselytising nor intermarrying with the Nandi on any significant scale. But the 'Arabs' and 'Sudanese' freely intermarried with Nandi, and from these marriages and a few converts are descended the present 100 or so Nandi Muslim families.

The earliest contact between the Nandi and Christians took place when missionary travellers traversed Nandi country on the journey inland to Uganda from the coast. Few, if any, made more than passing acquaintance with the 'wild and lawless Nandi'. The first encounter between the Nandi and Christian missions was with the Friends African Industrial Mission at Kaimosi on the border of Nandi country, about 20 miles south-west of Kapsabet. It was a tragic encounter, resulting in the death of one of the missionaries. The events leading up to and the details surrounding the death are not easily interpreted but the outcome can be readily assessed: there has never been any significant Friends missionary work among the Nandi.

In 1909, missionaries belonging to the Church Missionary Society arrived to evangelise the Nandi, but by 1912 they had left because, it is reported, the people of Nandi showed little desire for Christianity.[10] The mission site was later leased to the Africa Inland Mission. Neither its missionaries, however, nor those of the Roman Catholic Mill Hill Mission appear to have had much success, that is until individual Nandi were converted to Christianity while outside the District in the employ of government, army or settler.[11]

For Nandi traditionalists all of life is religious. Every aspect of the cultural framework, material, social and spiritual, is a closely integrated, direct response to the physical environment in which the people find themselves. Even today, after some fifty years of change, it is difficult to separate the 'sacred' from the 'profane'.

However, notwithstanding this pervasive nature of Nandi 'religion', it is possible to isolate a distinctive concept by which the Nandi seek to come to terms with the meaning of their existence. They have a word, *kiet*, signifying 'world' or 'order' but probably better translated 'nature'.[12] To understand the concept underlying this word unlocks the door to Nandi religion. *Nature* can be understood in the narrower sense of natural forces such as rain, thunder and lightning, or more commonly in the wider sense of 'Nature' with a capital 'N', signifying the 'balance of nature', 'world order' or 'cosmological balance'. In the 'natural' scheme of things the Nandi recognise what may be termed a hierarchy of personal and impersonal forces: God, the thunder-gods, the shades of the ancestors (or 'living dead'), magic, and medicine. God is called *Asis*, the indefinite form of the noun 'sun'; he is the beneficent creator, sustainer of life and arbiter of justice. Being associated with, or symbolised by the sun, he is the giver of light, rain and fertility. Moreover, he has many appellations, some of which by translation can be rendered 'the shining one', 'the holy one', 'the benefactor', 'the omnipotent' or 'the supernatural' and 'the protector'. The good and bad thunder-gods are allowed by *Asis* to send life-giving rain or destructive lightning. More important to daily behaviour and everyday living are the living dead. They act either in a beneficent or maleficent manner towards their descendants depending on how they are treated in this life and the next. Hence they must be placated when necessary, to restore order. Magic is widespread in Nandi and some of its perpetrators are greatly feared to this day. It is to be distinguished from medicine although both magical cures and herbal remedies can be employed simultaneously.

Every Nandi today, whether he calls himself Christian or traditionalist, Muslim or agnostic, belongs to more than one world — more than one order. Indeed, he may belong to as many as three: his own tradition, western culture and a particular Christian, Muslim or humanist allegiance.

NOTES

1 For up-to-date discussions of the Kalenjin and their origins see B.E. Kipkorir with F.B. Welbourn, *The Marakwet of Kenya*, Nairobi, 1973; Christopher Ehret, 'Linguistics as a Tool for Historians', in Bethwell A. Ogot (ed.), *Hadith 1*, Nairobi, 1968, pp. 119-33; 'Cushites and the Highland and Plains Nilotes to A.D. 1800', in B.A. Ogot (ed.), *Zamani: A Survey of East African History* (new edition), Nairobi, 1974, pp.150-69; *Southern Nilotic History: Linguistic Approaches to the Study of the Past*, Northwestern, 1971; G.W.B. Huntingford, 'The Peopling of the Interior of East Africa by its Modern Inhabitants', in R. Oliver and G. Mathew (eds.), *History of East Africa*, Vol. I, Oxford, 1963, pp. 74-8.

2 G.W.B. Huntingford, *The Southern Nilo-Hamites*, London, 1953, p. 19.

3 Meaning 'many words' and probably derived from the long deliberations which took place before the *Chemng'al* reached decisions. The Nandi were becoming notorious for raiding not only cattle but caravan parties.

4 Kipkorir and Welbourn, op. cit., p. 72; G.W.B. Huntingford, 'Introduction', in the second edition of A.C. Hollis, *The Nandi: Their Language and Folk-lore*, Oxford, 1969, p. xix.

5 For example, it was forbidden to take meat together with milk and if milk had been drunk no meat could be eaten for 24 hours and if meat

had been eaten no milk could be drunk for 12 hours; also milk could not be boiled for fear that the cow might go dry.

6 The 'neighbourhood' is *koret* and the council of elders *kokwet*; the linking of 'neighbourhoods' is *bororiet* and the grouping of these *emet*.

7 Laibon is the anglicised form of the Maasai word *oloiboni*, meaning 'seer' or 'ritual expert' and synonymous with the Nandi *Orgoiyot*.

8 The story is recounted in detail in A.T. Matson, *Nandi Resistance to British Rule 1890-1906*, Nairobi, 1972.

9 The clan is *oret*, the kindred group *tiliet*.

10 The *Church Missionary Society Report* 1912-13, pp. 71-2.

11 The story is fully told and documented in my thesis: 'Ritual Change among the Nandi: A Study of Change in Life-Crisis Rituals 1923-1973', Bristol University, 1976, ch. III, pp. 40-100, 'The Nandi and Christian Missions'. See also *ibid*, Appendix E, pp. 368-75, 'The Nandi and Islam'.

12 *Kiet* is explained by G.W.B. Huntingford in *The Nandi of Kenya*, London, 1953, pp. 123-30.

III. Between Three Worlds

The more I explored and the more I considered the Nandi situation, the more I was to become preoccupied with the particular question of the young person caught between different worlds and the general problem of society as a whole trying to come to terms with the pressures of rapid social change.

I was to meet the schoolboy who cried aloud in his agony: 'Who am I? I feel a nowhere person.' Who indeed? Unaware of his identity he lacked integration at a personal level.

I was to encounter the young woman, brought up in a Christian home, educated in a mission school, and at fourteen years of age waylaid by her grandmother, forcibly circumcised and married to a Muslim man whom she had never met. It was painful in the extreme to listen to the story of her subsequent life as she told how she tried to come to terms with her Christian education, her traditional circumcision and her unhappy marriage to a Muslim husband. After marriage, with her mother's encouragement, she had tried to complete her education. When I met her the marriage had broken down and she was back working for missionaries in order to raise money for the support of her children.[1]

I was to console the student whose father refused permission for her to marry a man belonging to a different ethnic group. In many ways the two were suitable partners: they were both well educated and practising Christians — in these two areas, at least, their worlds coalesced. Their parents, however, were worlds apart and so marriage was unthinkable.

I was to listen to missionaries exclaim in bewilderment on their return from the funeral of a church member who had hanged herself because her husband had threatened to take a young schoolgirl as his second wife. In this instance the woman had been caught between the demands of her Christian faith and the wishes of her 'traditionalist' husband.

The identity crisis, the conflict of loyalties had been aggravated, or so I was led to believe, by missionary opposition to certain aspects of Nandi culture. I therefore asked myself the question: 'How serious was this opposition? How extensive?' As I probed the subject I learnt that in Nandi it was aimed in the main at initiation rites, particularly at the female rite of clitoridectomy, but also at marriage customs. Indeed, there had taken place in Nandi, I discovered, in the 1920s, a minor circumcision controversy not unlike its more famous counterpart in Kikuyu.[2]

The year 1924 was, I came to understand, a year of crisis and the year 1926 a decisive turning-point for the Christian missionary enterprise in the area. Already, in 1923, an ominous note was being

12

sounded in the government records: 'The missionaries give no trouble except in the case of girls who are invariably claimed by their parents when the circumcision age is reached, however, a *modus vivendi* is generally reached.'[3] By 1924 the compromise was no more; the peace was shattered and controversy raged: 'The one mission in the district is the Africa Inland at Jebesas', wrote the official, 'At present the 2 women members remaining have been moved into Kapsabet there having been *a little trouble* owing to their attitude to the lawful guardians of marriageable girls. They make but little progress [italics mine].'[4]

For the missionaries, however, it was no small matter but rather one of survival. From my interviews with missionaries of the 1920s and 1930s still living and accessible, and from accounts received from the first Nandi converts (subsequently elders of the church) I am convinced that the early missionaries taught very strongly against clitoridectomy on two accounts.[5] Biblically, the custom was viewed as an infringement of St. Paul's teaching in his first letter to the Christians at Corinth (1 Cor. 7:18, 19, where he lays down the principle that a person uncircumcised at the time of his call to become a Christian should remain in that state). Medically, the operation was considered not only hygienically undesirable but harmful in its effects — an argument advanced earlier by the Church of Scotland missionaries in Kikuyu. In sum, to the Nandi elders an uncircumcised young woman was not a Nandi, while to the Christian missionaries clitoridectomy was incompatible with Christianity. If the church were to take root, then traditional circumcision of any kind, male or female, must go.

The events of 1924-6 can be reconstructed as follows. Finding the two lady missionaries alone and defenceless at Chebesas, the Nandi decided it was an opportune time to attack the mission and rescue their girls: 'Let us go and bring our children home to have them circumcised; the men have gone, the ladies have no strength' were the words quoted by one of my informants. The ladies, in a quandary as to what to do, eventually decided to evacuate the girls by night. Having made their way to the nearest railway station they boarded the train for another mission station in the adjoining Kipsigis territory. The few boys who remained, on being questioned the following morning, reported their whereabouts and a messenger was quickly despatched to inform the District Commissioner. He immediately sent for the ladies and girls concerned, offering them temporary quarters near the government offices in Kapsabet township.

The Nandi might be forgiven at this juncture for echoing the Kikuyu saying: 'There is no difference between the European and the missionary!'[6]

By 1925, the two ladies and their protégés were settled together with three new missionaries on a site at Namgoi near Kapsabet. There appeared to be every reason to be optimistic about the future: the government had lent support and would probably continue to do so if it were seen to be to their advantage. Hitherto, not much love had been lost between the two, particularly with regard to circumcision policy. So work commenced on new mission buildings, but as it happened, the test was yet to come.

One of the Nandi chiefs had a daughter (Leah Jeptorus) at the mission. She was of marriageable age, ready for circumcision and betrothal. No doubt her father wished to benefit from the cattle which he would obtain in payment of the bridewealth and so he decided to sue the mission for custody of his daughter. Wrote the District Commissioner of the time:

As reported by my predecessor there has been trouble in the case of girls with the Africa Inland Mission which is now situated in Kapsabet Station. A test case with the Supreme Court however should make the situation clear both to the Mission and the Nandi. The case in question will be heard at the next Sessions presumably in the month of January or February, 1926.[7]

The Annual Report for 1926 contains the verdict and continues the government polemic against mission attitudes to circumcision:

The test case brought by a Nandi against the Africa Inland Mission for custody of his daughter a minor was compounded by the defendants who paid dowry for the girl in stock! I question whether these people are making much headway ... Generally speaking the Nandi are opposed to all mission enterprise principally on account of the propaganda by native teachers to the effect that not only female, but male circumcision is sinful![8]

From this and other evidence it appears that the verdict was a compromise. The payment of bridewealth to the girl's father was to be guaranteed by the mission in the event of marriage while in future no girl could be forced to undergo circumcision when within bounds of the mission compound.

To this day the tensions remain. So far as I can ascertain, only the very early Nandi women converts remained uncircumcised. In theory, the present-day Africa Inland Church takes as strong a stand as ever against the female rite; in practice, most girls are circumcised in preparation for marriage. Only very recently, with the increasing influence of western education and culture, have Nandi girls begun to eschew clitoridectomy. For a time before the Second World War, it is true, a christianised version of the rite operated under the influence of a certain Fr. J. Kuhn of the Roman Catholic Mill Hill Mission and his Nandi catechist, Francis Arap Biama. Due to lack of support from, among others, the elders the experiment failed and only its vestiges remain in the form of a rite performed by Christian circumcisers. It was the traditional rite which persisted and developed, right down to the present day. Whatever changes might take place girls still needed to be prepared for marriage.

Missionary attitudes to the male rite appear to have been somewhat more ambivalent, becoming even more so over the years. We know that the early CMS missionaries, W.S. Syson and the Rev. J.S. Herbert, expressed disapproval of the 'licence' accorded Nandi warriors after initiation, and concluded that the Nandi had no system of morals.[9] Similarly, missionaries of the Africa Inland Mission so discouraged circumcision as to deter Nandi young men from attending their school with the result that the colonial administration was forced to open its own 'Nandi Industrial School' in the District in 1925.[10] When, however, Francis Arap Biama, Nandi Roman Catholic catechist, converted outside the District, joined this school as a tailor-instructor around 1926 he encouraged circumcision, albeit in its christianised version. Then and later it became apparent that the possible justification of male circumcision on medical grounds led to its continuance openly among Christian converts either in hospital or at the hands of Christian circumcisers.

Missionary opposition to Nandi marriage customs was in line with general mission policy at the time. Polygamy, it was believed, was incompatible with Christianity. Therefore, any polygamist desiring to be baptised was enjoined to put away all but his first wife. Moreover, missionaries belonging to the Africa Inland Mission encouraged divorce for new converts who desired Christian partners. Ironically, it was they who, at times, requested the District Commissioner's office to grant civil divorce to those married by Nandi customary law. This reflected their belief, reiterated in my hearing by an elderly missionary, that Nandi marriage was not 'marriage in the sight of God'. In yet another area the Nandi were to be caught between different worlds.

Against this background, I interviewed numerous Nandi (Christian, Muslim and traditionalist) and any available missionaries of all denominations. In addition, I collected and collated some fifty different accounts of each of the present-day rites of initiation, marriage and divorce, all in 1973. Furthermore, I cross-checked the male initiation rite with young instructors and attended a female circumcision festival. In the latter instance I discovered, with enormous interest, that the rite had not only persisted and developed in form and symbolism over the years, but it had become a potent symbol of 'Nandiness', an affirmation of what it meant historico-politically and socio-culturally to be a Nandi, while at the same time having little or no relevance, as an institution, for modern conditions of living.

What follows is a description of the rites of initiation (or, as I shall call them, *tumdo*[11]), marriage and divorce, their symbolism and development. It is based on accounts by contemporary participants, brought to life in the case of clitoridectomy by personal observation of the ceremony at Sang'alo in Central Nandi on 21-22 December 1973, and authenticated by Nandi elders.

From the description it will become clear that at least in one great event — *tumdo*, a potent symbol of 'Nandiness' — all worlds momentarily appear to converge. Every section of society has its role to play and its function to fulfil; the strains of change are forgotten and for one brief moment Nandi youth have an identity.

NOTES

1 The interview is transcribed in full on pp. 243-4 of my 'Ritual Change among the Nandi'.

2 From the earliest days missionaries of the Church of Scotland Mission in Kikuyu had taught against female circumcision. In March 1916 two church committees recommended that the circumcision of baptised girls or girls of Christian parents, or girls in mission boarding schools be made a matter for church discipline. In March 1929 the female circumcision rite was declared evil and all Christians submitting to it, it was decided, should be suspended by churches everywhere. A major crisis blew up as a result and a letter in the *East African Standard* of 29 August in the same year illustrates well the traditional Kikuyu reaction to the mission ban: 'For we feel', wrote Joseph Kang'ethe, President of the Kikuyu Central Association, 'it is an attempt to abolish an ancient custom and thus lead us into an avenue of general demoralisation of the ancestral tribal custom ... Missionaries have tried on many occasions to interfere with the tribal customs and the question is asked whether circumcision being the custom of the Gikuyu Christian, he is to be a heathen because he is a Gikuyu.'
   For a fuller discussion and bibliography see my 'Ritual Change among the Nandi', pp. 88-91.

3 Annual Report for 1923, in File No. DC/NDI/1/3, Kenya National Archives, Nairobi.

4 Annual Report for 1924, in File No. DC/NDI/1/3, Kenya National Archives, Nairobi.

5 For full documentation see my 'Ritual Change among the Nandi', pp. 87-8.

6 *Gutiri muthungu na mubia*, in Kikuyu.

7 Annual Report for 1925, in File No. DC/NDI/1/3, Kenya National Archives, Nairobi.

8 Annual Report for 1926, in File No. DC/NDI/1/3, Kenya National Archives, Nairobi.

9 See J.S. Herbert, in the *Church Missionary Society Report 1910-11*, pp. 475-6.

10 I reached this conclusion independently, only to find it confirmed in the Principal's Report, Nandi Industrial School, 1926 (File No. DC/NDI/3/1) where G.W.B. Huntingford writes:
   'Till 1924 the Nandi attitude was said to be hostile to education of any kind. What seems to have frightened them was the Christian religion, on the grounds that it would interfere with certain of their customs, e.g. circumcision, the importance of which to the tribe cannot be over-estimated. The Missions seem to have set their minds against circumcision, whether male or female. The question of the merits or demerits

of the latter is at present beside the point; all that can be said at present is that in order to get any sort of hold on this tribe all reference to circumcision is best omitted. This, I am convinced, is the reason why no Mission has yet been successful in Nandi.' See also my 'Ritual Change among the Nandi', pp. 60, 92.

11 *Tum* or *tumdo* is the Nandi for 'ceremony', particularly initiation ritual.

IV. Male Initiation

The supremely important moment in the life of a Nandi youth is the moment of circumcision. By means of the flick of a knife at the climax of a long ritual process boyhood becomes a thing of the past and manhood is entered. This I found to be no less true of the modern youth whom I taught in the 1960s and 1970s than of the young warrior encountered by A.C. Hollis when he travelled through Nandi at the turn of the century — that is, in theory. For in effect there is a profound difference between the rite as it was then and as it is now. Nowadays, the effect is largely illusory because today's youth is less likely to make an inner transition from one state to another than remain — possibly for the rest of his life — a 'threshold person' in the midst of a rapidly changing East African society.[1]

One of the continuing functions of Nandi male initiation is the perpetuation of the named age-set system, hence the need to understand something of its working before proceeding further.

There were seven age-sets and every set progressed to a new age-grade approximately every fifteen years. There were also seven age-grades through which a man passed during his life time — that is, in theory, for in practice there were really three — boys, warriors and elders. The length of the recurring cycle, as we have already mentioned, was about 105 years. Each set was further divided into sub-sets, of which there were four, although nowadays one often hears of three or even two — change having effected mergers.[2]

Initiation rituals used to take place over four successive years of the fifteen-year cycle. Members of each sub-set or *mat* were initiated together during one year and increasingly enjoyed a close relationship and strong social bond.[3] This bond was sustained through life and generally extended to all members of the same age-set.

The military significance of the age-set and age-grade system was that the Nandi always had a standing army. In attack and defence, in battle and in cattle-raiding, they had in constant readiness a fighting force composed mainly of the warriors in office but with the addition of members of the senior sub-set of the initiates and the younger of the junior elders. Further organisation of the force was based on the area territorial division.

1. *Timing*

Traditionally, the timing of *tumdo* was bound up intrinsically with the opening and closing of the generations, the handing over of guardianship to a new generation of warriors, and the flowering of a ritual plant. Various forces for change however — particularly government, mission and school — have combined to make certain of these factors obsolete, so that present day timing is altogether a different matter.

The ritual plant *setiot* (*mimulopsis* sp.) flowers in Nandi every six to eight years and in the past every alternate flowering marked the beginning of a new circumcision period, the initiation of the next age-set in the recurrent cycle.[4] Nowadays, however, although it remains true that the named age-set system regulates the timing of *tumdo* to some extent and the age-set system is in turn regulated by the flowering of the ritual plant, the flowering itself does not govern the timing of circumcision periods. Instead, they are governed to a considerable extent by school holidays. For example, the plant flowered in Nandi in 1926 and the boys of the Nandi Industrial School were given leave of absence from June for festivities which did not begin until October.[5] In 1947, however, the Local Native Council issued a statement proposing the month of December as a suitable time for circumcision leave.[6] Nowadays, schoolboys tend to be circumcised within the regular six-week December break, in any year, while boys who do not attend school go to *tumdo* during the months of March and August as well.

Seven to nine years after the flowering of the ritual plant it used to be reckoned to be time for the warriors in office to retire and hand over the guardianship of the people to a new generation. This handing over was marked by an elaborate ritual.[7] On orders from the chief ritual expert, the *Laibon*, all adult members belonging to the incoming and outgoing age-sets gathered in one place. A white bullock was slaughtered and the meat divided and eaten by the elders of the senior age-set while small rings from its hide were made by the warriors belonging to the incoming age-set and placed, one each, on a finger of the right hand. Before their departure, the outgoing warriors divested themselves of warriors' clothing, putting on instead the fur garments proper to their new-found elders' status, while the incoming warriors were charged by the *Laibon* with protecting the countryside and seeing to the welfare of its inhabitants. The handing over ritual was last held in 1892/3 because of the ban imposed by the colonial government.

Two to four years after the handing over, as the end of a circumcision period drew near, three age-grades made the inauguration of a new period their concern. These were the incoming elders, the incoming warriors and the up-and-coming initiands. It fell to the senior sub-set of the incoming warriors to tell their counterpart among the incoming elders that the ritual plant had flowered. This announcement was then followed by a meeting in each area.[8] At this meeting two representatives were chosen from among the platoon commanders belonging to the senior sub-set of the incoming warriors.[9] It was then their responsibility to choose two heifers from among the cattle belonging to men of their own age-set. The heifers, with beer already prepared by the fathers of the up-and-coming initiands, were

intended as gifts for the *Laibon*. On receiving the gifts he was expected
to sanction the opening of the new circumcision period. An inauguration ritual, called *kigulei kwet* (literally, 'we bleed the goat') was then
held in every area. The people assembled for a day and as the elders
drank beer goats were killed and their meat eaten by the up-and-
coming initiands. There is a tradition which says that the goats'
entrails were examined and ritual plants burnt in the fire by representatives of the different clans to judge the omens. If the entrails were
satisfactory and the auspices favourable the plants were placed on the
fire. If the ascending smoke went directly upward into the clear and
still morning air then all was reckoned to be well. *Asis* was thought to
have accepted the prayers of the people for a good beginning to a new
generation. [10]

In 1926 the inauguration ritual was held in June and *tumdo* began
in October, presumably with the *Laibon*'s sanction. In 1941 representatives from all areas met together in June to discuss the opening of the
new circumcision period. There is no mention of asking for the
Laibon's sanction. Indeed, it would have been contrary to government
policy to have done so. The new period began in August 1942 and, to
the best of my knowledge, the inauguration ritual has not been held
since. It is not necessary, since, nowadays, *tumdo* takes place annually,
mainly in December, but also, as we saw, in March and August. It is
held after discussion between boys and parents and between parents
and neighbourhood elders, and not by sanction of the *Laibon*.
Candidates are usually quite young, between twelve and fifteen years
of age on average.

2. *Preparation*[11]

When elders, parents and boys have agreed to hold a circumcision
festival parents and elders set about choosing two 'sponsors' and a
'master of ceremonies'.[12] The two sponsors must belong to the
warrior grade, and are normally chosen from among members of the
age-set immediately senior to that of the initiands.[13] They must be
well-versed in Nandi lore, well-respected and married with a family,
the first born of which has to be a boy. It is the sponsors' duty to
instruct the candidates before and after the operation and maintain a
special relationship with them throughout life. The master of
ceremonies must be a ritual expert and he is normally chosen from
among the junior elders. It is his duty to supervise all details pertain-
ing to the ritual. Both the sponsors and the master of ceremonies are
given due reward for their services.

Tumdo is the event of the year in every neighbourhood, but nowadays, only two or three boys go forward for initiation at any one time,
under the care of one pair of sponsors.[14]

It is now the turn of parents, sponsors and master of ceremonies to choose a time and place for *tumdo*. The obvious choice with regard to time is a week-end in December: week-ends are the times when relatives and friends come home from town and city and are free to relax with feasting, singing and dancing; December is a month of plenty (food is still most plentiful from October onwards) and holiday (December is part of the long school vacation). The venue is a matter for negotiation between parents and elders. If a dwelling house of suitable size is not available to serve as the 'house of *tumdo*' then the community erects a special building for the occasion. It is often supplemented by a canvas-topped or thatched marquee-like structure in which visitors may shelter from the midday sun.

The preparation includes all the practical preparations undertaken by women as well as men and candidates. Three weeks, or maybe as long as three months, beforehand the women start collecting milk, storing it in large gourds placed in a special compartment of the house. There, it is allowed to ferment, to be used later for the feeding of the initiands after their operation. Often, however, nowadays, fresh milk with a little charcoal flavouring is preferred to the fermented *mursik*.[15] Nearer the time, the women are to be seen taking maize and millet to the mill for grinding. The maize is used to make beer and stiff porridge for the feast and gruel with which to feed the initiands during their period of seclusion.[16] Other preparations involving the women of the household, kindred group and neighbourhood are daubing the house of *tumdo* and decorating its exterior with red and white clay.

In all the preparations reinforcement of Nandi social organisation and division of labour may be observed. Boys, warriors and elders have their distinctive roles to play; so too have men and women. But perhaps most important are the distinctions made between circumcised and uncircumcised and between male and female.

Following the practical preparations comes the 'announcing and sending out of the good news about *tumdo*'.[17] *Tumdo* is a secret ritual and, apart from the initiands, only Nandi males and childless women may be present for the entire proceedings. Women and children, however, may attend the public singing and dancing and therefore invitations are issued to a large number of relatives and friends and neighbours. All members of the kindred group both near and far must be invited, together with members of the neighbourhood. In the past, the candidates dressed especially for this event in long headdresses made of grasses. Nowadays, they go about in everyday clothing, usually an open-necked shirt and a pair of shorts. Neighbours are invited partly because they give help and bring presents. Everybody is told the time and place of the important event.

The announcement is often accompanied by singing. Indeed, songs are practised for the dance to be held on the evening prior to the operation. In the particular song following, the singer is praising his

father, recounting to Sindala all the good things his father did for him
when he was young.

Refrain
   Sindala, my father loved me when I was young.

   Sindala, my father loved me when I was young;
   Agree, it is nice.
   Sindala, he pierced part of my ear;
   Agree, it is nice.
   Sindala, ee — oh — oh — O Sindala;
   Agree, it is nice.

Refrain
   Sindala, my father loved me when I was young.

   Sindala, my father loved me when I was young;
   Agree, it is nice.
   Sindala, he bought me clothing like this;
   Agree, it is nice.
   Sindala, ee — oh — oh — O Sindala;
   Agree, it is nice.

Refrain
   Sindala, my father loved me when I was young.

   Sindala, my father loved me when I was young;
   Agree, it is nice.
   Sindala, he bought me a belt like this;
   Agree, it is nice.
   Sindala, ee — oh — oh — O Sindala;
   Agree, it is nice.

Then, two to seven days before *tumdo* proper it is usual for the boys
to return to their homes and take the first important step in the initiation ritual. This is the building of the circumcision or seclusion
lodge.[18] It is not only an act of obvious practical significance but also
one which possesses ritual value. The candidates together with their
brothers and certain members of their own age-set go with their
sponsors to a relatively inaccessible and hidden site not too far from
the house of *tumdo* (or their homes) — by the bank of a stream in the
forest or in the dense undergrowth along its edge. Here, they make a
clearing and set about building, of sticks and grass, a small undaubed
one-roomed hut to serve as a circumcision lodge. On its completion it
is surrounded by a fence which provides protection and camouflage.[19]

   Following is an account of the building of a circumcision lodge
given me by two young men initiated together in December 1972 and
currently assisting in the training of new initiands belonging to their
age-set.

   About 10 a.m. on the Friday morning candidates and their age-
mates proceed with their two sponsors and the master of ceremonies

to the site chosen for the circumcision lodge. Here, in order to symbolise the close relationship to be forged between sponsors and initiands, they attempt together to fell a ritual tree,[20] holding the axe or broad-bladed knife in the following manner.[21] The inner part of the handle (nearest the blade) is held by the senior sponsor, the outer by the junior sponsor and the centre by the candidate.[22] Then, in order of seniority — arranged according to their fathers' age-set or sub-set[23] — the candidates strike the tree four times while singing the song known as *aiywet:*[24]

Oo — oo — oo — o — aiywa — eee — eee

The symbolic act completed, all help in cutting wood for the building of the circumcision lodge and return to the site. Here, a hole is made in the ground for the centre post and lined with Kikuyu grass, whereupon the master of ceremonies takes his small ritual gourd and expectorates beer from its side into the hole.[25] This moment of prayer and blessing over, the candidates, again in order of seniority, take hold of the centre post (in the same manner as they took hold of the axe) and place it in the hole. The action is repeated four times.

There are variations in procedural details at this point, some informants reporting, for example, a symbolic rather than an actual felling of the tree on the morning or evening of the first day of *tumdo*. However, the emphasis on the symbolic act of 'togetherness' or 'unitedness' remains.

On returning with their sponsors from the circumcision lodge candidates go to their homes where they may spend anything from a few hours to several days, depending on when they set out to build the lodge in the first place and how long the effort took.

Then, on the evening prior to the main ritual events, they leave their homes again and accompanied by sponsors, fathers, age-mates and maybe some elders, go to the home of the master of ceremonies. Here, during the night, and at the circumcision lodge next morning, ordeals and testings begin. The candidates are warned of such although they are not given precise details as to their nature. They are spoken to of 'fire' and 'water'. While standing by the fire circumcision will 'happen', so they are informed. The water they drink will be sweetened with honey. In reality, the 'fire' is the knife of circumcision and the 'water' the bitter herbal drink and ice-cold water splashed over the wound in the early hours of the following morning. Following this the candidates for initiation are put through some exercises of concentration similar to those which will take place next day.

From the region of the circumcision lodge the company collects firewood and ritual plants, particularly *sinendet*, a ritually significant creeper. Some of the firewood is left at the lodge and the remainder taken in procession to the house of *tumdo*. Like all others at *tumdo* this procession is formed strictly according to Nandi rules of seniority. It is led by the senior sponsor who is followed by the candidates, placed according to the order of their fathers' age-sets, while the junior sponsor brings up the rear. The ritual plants are used in building a shrine.[26]

3. *Shaving the Head*

At about 10 a.m., after the shrine has been erected, the boys' clothes are taken away and their heads shaved with razor blades by the sponsors. This takes place at the shrine and the shaven hair is either placed in cowdung and smeared around the base of the shrine or thrown towards the rising sun. This act embraces prayers to *Asis* for an auspicious beginning to *tumdo*. Meanwhile, the boys' heads are anointed four times — a sign of blessing — with milk from a little ritual gourd, and their bodies are smeared with red ochre or white clay mixed with milk for easy application.[27] It is applied with three fingers on head, face, arms and legs, making a pattern of two sets of three parallel lines — \\\ ///. Red signifies 'normality', white 'abnormality'. For example, a boy in whose family the child immediately preceding him died is smeared with white clay. Also, after shaving, the boys are given a strong purge made from one of three particular trees,[28] clothed in a short skin garment,[29] and garlanded by the senior sponsor with the *sinendet* creeper. From this moment onwards, the candidates are *tarusiek* — initiands, 'liminal creatures', 'people of transition', neither boys nor man. Technically, the transitional phase of the rite has begun.

While the men have been so occupied, the women will have been extremely busy attending to domestic duties. Relatives, friends and neighbours will have brought milk, beer, maize flour, vegetables and meat dishes, and a meal will be ready for the initiands in the house of *tumdo*.

4. *Transvestiture*

As will become clear virtually nothing survives today of transvestiture in the male rite. What happened traditionally is described by A.C. Hollis as follows:

After being shaved the boys are given a strong purge ... During the course of the morning warriors visit the *menjet* huts and seize and take away with them all the boys' clothes and ornaments. Young girls next pay them a visit, and give them some of their own garments ... and ornaments. Having attired themselves in these, the boys, who now receive the name of *tarusiek* (s. *tarusiot*), start off to inform their maternal uncles and other relations living in the neighbourhood that they are going to be circumcised and invite them to be present. If they have no maternal uncle living, a maternal cousin may take his place. Without the sanction of a maternal uncle or his representative no operation can be performed.

The next day dances are held which are called *cheptilet* and *aiyuet*. The boys are still dressed as girls and wear a bunch of *sinendet* in their ears ... When the boys have been passed by the warriors, their girl friends give them bead neck-laces to wear. Favourites are often smothered with strings of beads.[30]

Only the latter part of this custom continues today in the part of the ritual which is concerned with 'encouragement'.

5. *The Dance*

The next stage of *tumdo* is generally called *cheptilet* (literally, 'the cutting'). *Cheptilet* specifically refers to a dance and probably derives its name from the ritual felling of the tree. It has come, however, to be loosely used to denote that part of the ceremony which also encom-passes the repetition of the *aiywet* (literally, 'the axe') song, the testing of the initiands at *kabonyony* (literally, 'the place of testing'), and *cherset* (literally, 'the encouragement').

No longer are initiands dressed by girls before the dance. Instead, they remain in their skin garments, observed only by their sponsors. Distinctions in manner of dress are to be accounted for by differing personal circumstances. For example, clothing differs from clan to clan and according to whether an initiand is an only son or the younger son of a family in which a previous child has died.

Any time between 2 p.m. and 5 p.m. — the precise time depends on the heat of the afternoon sun — the guests invited to *tumdo* gather in a large clearing about 500 yards from the circumcision lodge and maybe 900 yards from the house of *tumdo*. The location of this clear-ing in relation to the house of *tumdo* depends on the distance between the latter and the circumcision lodge. While the guests thus assemble, the sponsors arrange the initiands in ritual order in readiness for a procession, and the young warriors prepare a clearing by the river and in close proximity to the circumcision lodge, designating it the 'place of testing'.[31]

The procession of initiands, led by the senior sponsor (the junior bringing up the rear), then moves away from the house of *tumdo*. As it nears the clearing it is met by numerous guests, old men, women and children, who thereupon form a circle with a shield and song leader in the centre. Men, carrying sprigs of the *acacia* and *cassia* species, form the inner circle and women the outer.[32] The song-leader, or soloist, then strikes up the song of the axe, followed by the dance during which the men sing and dance slowly and rhythmically following one behind the other, unlinked, in a circle. As they dance, the women accompany them, singing the songs of encouragement to help their young men through the ordeals yet to come. Then, suddenly and unexpectedly as it were, the rhythm changes as the song of the axe is struck up once again. This is the signal for women to withdraw 4 yards away, so allowing the procession of initiands — led by the senior sponsor and closed by the junior sponsor — to pass through on the way to the place of testing. Only women afflicted by barrenness and numerous deaths among brothers and sisters may accompany the procession. At the place of testing, called in Nandi *kabonyony*, the initiands are tested for bravery and concentration and given some instruction in the events of the next day. Probably, as a preliminary, they are shown a bow and arrows, a spear, a shield, in short all kinds of traditional weapons and are asked to confess any wrongs committed. The warriors administer various kinds of testing which differ from one occasion of *tumdo* to another. I enumerate a few below, the first — so far as I can ascertain — being the only one common to all occasions of *tumdo*.

The initiand is held from behind by one of his age-mates, while another comes towards him with a spear which is thrust near his face. He must look directly at the warrior holding the spear, without blinking, while others try to distract his attention.

The initiand is shown a piece of wood, approximately 2 feet by 3 feet in dimension and with a hole 2 inches in diameter in the centre. It is placed about 50 yards away and the initiand is told that he must shoot an arrow through the centre hole.

The initiand is asked to pass through a 'goal post' formed of three small sticks and about 6 inches high. If in any way he shows hesitation he is laughed and jeered at and told to prove his manhood by 'passing through'.

The initiand stands while an age-mate pretends to attack his penis with a wooden knife. On this occasion he must not blink.

Every test is repeated four times and all failure is greeted with mockery.

To conclude the session a very old man, well-experienced in circumcision ritual, leads the singing of an incantation. Its aim is to invoke the curse on any uncircumcised person or woman who might be

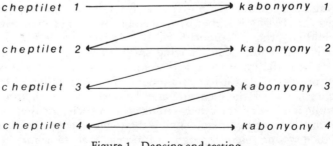

Figure 1. Dancing and testing

secretly lurking in the bush.[33] One form invokes sterility on the woman: 'Woman, get dry and may your neck be white.'

The procession then wends its way back to the clearing for another session of song and dance. In fact, both the dancing and the testing are repeated four times. The fourth time round brings both the dancing and the testing to their climax.

6. *Encouragement*[34]

Among the women, in particular, tension and excitement have been mounting; so much so that they shout and jump, weep and faint in the process. At last, they are allowed to break the circle and gain access to the initiands for the purpose of encouraging them, called in Nandi *cherset*. Shouting words of encouragement and abuse (all with the same intent of giving the initiands courage and determination for the coming ordeal) they drape the 'boys' with beaded necklaces and belts and head-squares divested from their own persons and bedeck them with ornaments such as bells. Some of their words are positive and encouraging:

'Do not fear circumcision; if this were death how many people have gone through it?'
'Nothing will harm you, may you give your body to have anything done to it — that which remains will be yours.'

Others are negative and abusive, overstepping the bounds of sex and propriety:

'You wife of a shade!'[35]

'I am not prepared to get married to someone who is a coward and if you know that you will cry tell me so that I may look for someone else.'

Mothers in particular weep for their sons. The crying is called *siet* in Nandi and was aptly described for me by a schoolgirl. The women's actions, as she puts it, add a feeling to the ritual at this point — a feeling that a stage has been gone through:

As you know, mothers always get too excited for nothing ... they are anxious on these occasions and sometimes they will weep when they think of their little boys becoming men just as they do at weddings. Sometimes because it signifies that the children are growing apart from them and becoming independent. They will no longer be their little sons but men and will sleep in separate huts after the ceremony to show that they are no longer considered as children.

During all this time the men continue their singing and dancing unabated. The songs are special to *tumdo* and secret.[36] Boys and initiands are being trained in their content and use. However, on the way from the dance to the place of testing the initiands sing simple songs of initiation like this:

SOLOIST: I will go, warriors, I fear nothing.
PEOPLE: *Aleyo toleiyoi ee.*

Or, while dancing in a circle they sing this:

Arap Tormoi eh! The cattle have come back; x 2
They have come back with one that is not black. x 4
Arap Tormoi eh! The cattle have come back; x 2
They have come back with one that has a white neck. x 4
Arap Tormoi eh! The cattle have come back; x 2
They have come back with one that is brownish. x 4

It is about 7 p.m. now and after the encouragement the procession moves for the fourth and final time to the place of testing. If the initiands have not already been fed at the house of *tumdo* they are now fed with blood, milk and porridge, or nowadays, even with meat, and given some rest at the circumcision lodge. Afterwards, they are taken into the darkness outside and subjected to further testing. They are told to gaze at the stars without blinking. Stars are needed for circumcision and if they blink the stars will not fall. While thus gazing unsuspectingly into the heavens they are crept up on by stealthy warriors who apply nettles to their genitals.[37] The process of 'anaesthetising' the body has begun.

Meanwhile, the elders are clearing the house of *tumdo* and preparing it for the night-long proceedings yet to come.

7. *The 'Anointing'*[38]

When the house of *tumdo* has been set in order and the initiands are sufficiently rested — anytime between 8 p.m. and midnight, depending on when the dance got under way — the women are summoned for the last time to the scene of the activities. The initiands, with their sponsors, stand in ritual order by the shrine while female relatives, specially chosen to represent the clan and kindred group of each initiand, arrive to anoint them. Nowadays, this ritual is performed in either of two ways, one obviously a time-saving abbreviated form of the other. The appointed woman stands by the shrine and takes clarified butter (or, as it is known colloquially, 'oil from the teats of a cow'), with a stick used normally for cleaning gourds, from a small decorated ritual ox-horn, and proceeds to smear it on the face, chest and legs of the senior sponsor, initiand and junior sponsor, in that order.[39] She performs the anointing four times and spits once in blessing. From this time onwards a special relationship will exist between the initiand and this woman — each will address the other as *bamwai*. Alternatively, the appointed female relative dispenses the clarified butter from the ox-horn, with the cleaning stick, to all female relatives, women, girls and children alike, in chronological order, and they in turn anoint the sponsors and the initiand. I repeat, only the female members of the initiand's clan and kindred group perform this act.

Finally, before their dismissal, the women chant a prayer of blessing, requesting 'deft hands' for the operators and 'strong hearts' for the initiands, while the initiands circumambulate the shrine four times.

8. *Ordeals*

While waiting outside the house of *tumdo* the initiands are again put through the ordeal of star-gazing, accompanied by the application of nettles. Until after the actual operation is over and the period of seclusion has begun, veiled language only is used by the master of ceremonies, the sponsors, elders, and warriors engaged in the ritual proceedings.[40]

From this point onwards, after the banishment of the women, only traditionally- (that is, fully-) initiated Nandi men and the categories of women already mentioned are allowed to be present. Intruders may find themselves punished by a fourfold application of the nettle! However, in rare circumstances, a male stranger who agrees to the ritual application of the nettle may be granted permission to remain for the whole of *tumdo*.

While the initiands are thus engaged in 'star-gazing', the elders inside the house of *tumdo*, led by the master of ceremonies and the sponsors, erect the *kimusanyit* structure. This is a table-like arch covered on its two sides and top and open at both ends and erected facing east in the animal compartment of the house. Each side and the top are constructed of either four or eight poles of *markhamia platacalyx* species, as illustrated.

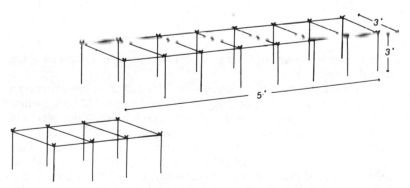

Figure 2. Erection of the *kimusanyit* arch

No other type of wood may be used. Neither nails nor knots are employed in securing the poles; they are bound with ropes of a ritual creeper.[41] It is essential that the structure is sturdy enough to bear the weight of a man. The top and sides are then covered with nettles and finally the top is overlaid with the skin garments of the initiands. The general term applied in referring to the structure is *kimusanyit*, although as the events of the night proceed, it becomes successively 'a cow' and 'an elephant's stomach'. Probably it bears other designations as well, but these are the only two which I have recorded. The top of the arch is given right and left sides. The right is male and the left female. On the right are placed implements used by and important to men; on the left are those used by women and with which men ought to be familiar. Nowadays, it is becoming increasingly difficult to acquire all the necessary implements, and many are missing from the various ceremonies. In addition, each corner has a stick for cleaning gourds attached, while in the centre atop is a large gourd decorated with cowries and used specifically by warriors. Along the centre of the top and dividing right from left is a leather strap used to tether a cow while it is being bled, with a gourd dangling from one end and a cowbell from the other.[42] The arch can be illustrated in the following manner:

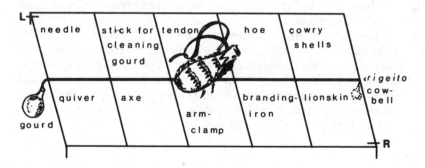

Figure 3. The *kimusanyit* structure

As an alternative arrangement the implements may be placed along the sides.

Atop this structure sits *Musanyit* — an elder in the nude, ringing a bell for the initiands to enter. They enter one by one, led by a sponsor or alternatively all together in ritual order, each holding the person in front. (It is the sponsors who decide which of the two procedures is chosen.) As the bell rings, elders and warriors sing special songs, some stereo-typed and unintelligible, others comparatively new and yet others composed especially for the occasion, but all paying respect to the great institution of *tumdo* and the wisdom of the ancestors.[43]

When the singing has been repeated four times, the first initiand, in the nude, led by a sponsor (still dressed!), begins the procession through the arch. Warriors stand at the entrance, at the exit, and along the sides of the structure waiting to apply nettles to the initiands' bare bodies. Others have cold water ready to pour on the smarting flesh. Each initiand goes through four times and when he does so he is stung particularly on the face and genitals, and dowsed with cold water. The water serves to increase the pain. The arch or 'animal' is variously termed 'cow' or 'elephant's stomach' at this juncture. I am told that 'abusive' language is used also:

The boys are regarded as cattle. They are to get in as cows and the language used is abusive (only circumcised men are present). The *motiriot* tells the young men 'Get through the vagina of an elephant, if it stings don't scratch yourself, that is very bad.' ... The members of the crowd whistle as they do to the cows from the river.

'Do not be afraid, it [water] is only elephant's urine.'

The ordeal bravely endured, the initiands are told by the old man, *Musanyit*, that they must be shown the circumcision started by *Mong'o*, long ago. In turn, they are asked to identify the various implements to the elders' satisfaction, and instructed in the building of the arch. Following this, they circumambulate the structure four times, dancing and singing, finally stamping on the top. It may be that they begin its dismantling in this manner.

Outside, once again, the initiands resume 'star-gazing'; this time they themselves apply nettles to their own genitals, while sitting straddle-legged and almost naked on the ground, in the cold air of a Kenya highlands night. Some informants report that rest and food — milk, blood and millet porridge — follow, others that neither food nor sleep is allowed all night long. Certainly, by this time, pain and discomfort are so great that the climax is anticipated with some eagerness and urgency!

Meanwhile, inside the house of *tumdo*, a simple structure of sticks and skins has been erected to the left of the door as one enters the animal compartment, and a fire kindled to the right. The purpose of this second structure is simply to act as a camouflage for the fierce growling 'animal' called *Kimasop*. In reality, *Kimasop* is an old man dressed in a colobus monkey skin cloak or lionskin and playing a friction drum.[44] By drawing his hands up and down (in the manner of milking a cow) on an oiled stick standing at the centre of the top of the drum he simulates a roaring animal.

Now, one by one, the initiands enter to request circumcision: 'I have called my relatives, I have built a circumcision lodge, please be kind to me, give me *tumdo* and I will give you a cow and a half', or words to this effect, they repeat. It is *Kimasop*'s job, however, to extract confession of wrongdoing before giving his consent. Specific questions are asked, mainly concerning illicit sex and stealing.

Asked if he has conducted himself improperly with any woman, circumcised or uncircumcised, married or unmarried, the initiand at first answers 'No'. But *Kimasop* will not readily take 'No' for an answer and warns the initiand of the consequences of unconfessed wrongdoing — failure to bear up at *tumdo* or failure of the wound to heal afterwards. If guilty, the initiand is frightened and answers in the affirmative, whereupon he is asked to reveal the woman's identity. If he denies any such transgression the old man proceeds to stir a stick noisily in a pot filled with mud from the river, saying: 'The whole multitude shouts that this initiand had a woman in the swamp down there, you can hear the noise of this thing. Don't laugh, tell about the woman.' The action is repeated four times while the initiand kneels before the old man, his head being held low by a sponsor. Then, surreptitiously, some millet, salt or a twig of the crackly *lippia javanica* species is thrown on the fire, the noise being intended to indicate the displeasure of the shades.[45] Truth must be told. Still more confession is required. Has he stolen maize? Then it must be returned, and so on. Moreover, the initiand's agony is increased, as all this time the master of ceremonies has been sharpening the circumcision knife in the living quarters next door.[46]

Finally, more objects are brought for identification: a three-legged stool and three sticks standing in the form of a goal post in cowdung by the fire. The latter must be identified as a cattle gate through which cows, sheep, goats and shepherds pass. The elders in the living room then affirm their satisfaction and the initiand is allowed to repeat finally his request for *tumdo*, indicating this time that he is ready, if necessary, to go through a bloody ordeal. In reply, *Kimasop* cups his hands and blows into a little pot, saying 'Boo — oo — oo — oo', signifying 'Yes'.

Some variations in detail may occur on different occasions of *tumdo*, due in some instances to differences of clan or area, but the general pattern of the major events is stereo-typed.[47]

9. *Circumcision*[48]

It is 2 a.m. or later when the circumcision knife is sharpened and water, honey, medicine and other accoutrements are prepared, in readiness for the operation at dawn. Then, after 4 a.m. the initiands move in procession to the river to bathe, and from thence to the circumcision lodge for the final application of nettles. Meanwhile, their age-mates and the young warriors have gathered in the clearing near the circumcision lodge to light a large fire, and their mothers, with the rest of the women and children, have arisen with the first cock-crow and gathered in the open place where the dance was held the evening before.

1. Nandi warriors, c.1905.

2. Nandi warriors, 1973.

Above: 3. Initiands in
seclusion, 1973.

Right: 4. Initiand in ritual
headdress and women's garb,
*c.*1905.

The sound of singing just before dawn signals the arrival of the elders from the house of *tumdo*. By the light of the fire they watch while the initiands are subjected to their final testing; once again, faced with a spear, they must stare at it without blinking. Then as the sun begins to rise a circle is formed and the initiands line up in ritual order headed by their leader, the 'firstborn'. Any unauthorised person lurking nearby is cursed with the threat of death and the special songs of circumcision are begun. The initiands are seated, naked, on leaves of *veronia auriculifera* species,[49] each firmly holding his own penis while he is held down from behind by one age-mate and faced with a spear by another.[50]

While the initiand's gaze is thus fixed on the spear (tree or bush) he is approached by the master of ceremonies. Drawing one hand slowly over the initiand's eyes the master of ceremonies deftly cuts and severs the foreskin which has been drawn forward over the tip of the glans. The successful completion, that is the initiand's endurance of the pain, without crying or flinching, of this first or symbolical stage of 'cutting' is greeted with great excitement by the relatives and friends of each initiand. As the singing of the special circumcision songs signifies the completion of this stage the young warriors run with branches of the *sinendet* creeper to waiting women and children. If the creeper is tied in long and loose bunches, success is indicated and great rejoicing is engaged in: shouts of excitement rend the air while men and women are swept off their feet in embrace. If, on the other hand, the creeper is tied in short small bunches or burnt at its tips, it indicates failure; the boy concerned is called *kibite* — coward — and forbidden to attend any future ceremonies while his relatives go to their homes in disgrace without bidding farewell. This latter is rare and usually the relatives return home with bunches of the ritual creeper to tie on the rooftops, thus proclaiming to the whole neighbourhood the initiand's bravery and capacity for endurance.

Certainly, when A.C. Hollis wrote, there were two distinct stages to the operation, even as there are today in many instances. Nowadays, however, it is common to treat endurance of the final testing administered before dawn on the morning of the operation as equivalent to going through the symbolic 'cutting' and circumcision itself is then performed by an 'expert' such as 'Jimmy' (the first Nandi medical assistant),[51] and not necessarily by the master of ceremonies or a sponsor in the traditional mould. Moreover, if the initiands cry aloud in pain the volume of singing is increased so that the waiting women and children cannot hear.

When all the initiands have been circumcised the sponsor operating calls out '*Iy — ae — ee — ee ...* ' and the crowd replies '*Ari — ri — ri — ri ...* ', a form of blessing including the waving of the ritual creeper.

At this point I should like to supplement my own account by

quoting *verbatim* two of my informants who must remain anonymous and also A.C. Hollis:

The old man called *boiyob tum* goes in front, another follows holding a spear and the boy looks at him. The old man brings his hand slowly over the eyes to make the boy blink. Then the knife is brought out and a bit of the foreskin cut, while someone behind is holding, and the boy looks aside immediately. This is to show he has undergone circumcision. All go through this. All the people come together and bring *sinendet* creeper from the bush. This is the operation undergone symbolically. A sign is given and all the people go to the clearing, they meet women and children and give them creeper to show that they have undergone circumcision without crying. There is great excitement now that the sons are men and no longer children, although the major part of the operation has not yet been undergone.

Now, they come by again and this time the boys are given people who know how to operate. They are taken aside completely naked, the one who holds is behind, the one who operates in front. The skin of the glans is cut and all removed. This is very painful and honey is drunk while the boy looks up and water is poured on the bloody penis. The boy goes on kicking while people hold him down. The difference between the traditional and the hospital operation is that the Nandi believe that when a man gets married his penis may be weak and so they make it more erect by a further operation. A small hole is made in the skin and it is pulled tightly while the glans is pulled through. The tension of the skin makes the penis look upright.

It is very cold then, and two sticks are brought and the boy while sitting down holds the sticks, because of the cold and shivering. They are told that old men and women are abusing them … All come and spit on the young men wishing them well. If the penis is swelling [aside, 'not a good operation!'] then this is taken to mean that the boy has slept with somebody's wife, and he hasn't admitted it. (I got on all right, but the boy next to me was ill throughout his stay. The operator wanted two shillings for a drink as penalty, and tried to persuade the boy to confess [his unconfessed transgressions]. The *motirēnik* tried to no avail as the boy knew that it was a badly done job.) The stay was six weeks and the boys were fed on milk, blood and *posho*.[52]

Veiled or enigmatic language is used throughout, for example, when the *tarusiot* is about to be 'cut': 'See a girl coming with a big red neck' — describing the penis.[53]

At that hour the warriors and old men collect together round the *menjet* huts, the boys are brought out, and at sunrise the operation commences. All weapons must be removed to a distance, and nobody may speak. The boy to be operated on stands up and is supported by the senior *moteriot* from behind. The other boys with the junior *moteriot* sit in a line close by, looking on. The operator, who is called *poiyot-ap-tum*, kneels in front of the boy, and with a deft cut of the *kipōs* performs the first part of the operation, the foreskin being drawn forward and severed just in front of the tip of the glans penis. The boy's face is carefully watched by the surrounding crowd of warriors and old men to see whether he blinks or makes a sign of pain. Should he in any way betray his feelings, he is dubbed a coward and receives the nickname of *kipite*. This is considered a great disgrace, and no *kipite* may ever attend another circumcision festival or be present at children's dances. Those boys that are brave receive presents of bunches of *sinendet* from the women, who greet them with cries of joy when they hand the bead necklaces they received after the *kâponyony* ceremony back to their girl friends. The foreskins are collected by the old men, who pour milk and beer on them and put them away in an ox-horn. This done, all the friends and relations make merry whilst the second part of the operation is performed, at which only barren women and women who have lost several brothers or sisters in quick succession may be present. The skin of the penis is retracted well back, and the inner covering of the glans is slit up, peeled off, and cut away behind the corona. The skin is next pulled tightly over the glans, and a transverse slit is made on its dorsal surface about half an inch long and about the same distance from its bleeding edge. Through this slit the glans is pushed, and the final stage of the operation is the trimming away of the resulting pucker of skin thus formed. During this part of the operation many boys collapse from the pain. Only cold water is administered to the lacerated parts, after which the boys are taken by their *motērenik* to the *menjet* hut, where they live quietly for the next few weeks.[54]

The operation over, the initiands are taken to the circumcision lodge where they are clothed in girls' skin garments, fed with milk, blood and a light porridge made of finger millet. Medicine is applied to the wound. In the past, traditional medicine only was allowed, nowadays, iodine and various antiseptics and antibiotics are commonly employed.[55]

10. *The Washing of Hands*[56]

For a period of four or six days the initiands are made to rest completely.[57] During this period they must not eat with their hands because of ritual uncleanness.[58] Food is eaten with a small wooden knife or a stick — *seget* — from a piece of curved wood, a strip of bark or a half calabash. At no time, even after the washing of hands ceremony, are plates, knives, forks or spoons employed for eating. Milk, water and porridge are taken cold at this time and nowadays are supplemented by bottles of Fanta and Coca-Cola! As strength returns to the initiands meat is added to their diet and, contrary to normal custom, may be taken with milk at this time. The parents of the initiands arrange a rota, feeding their sons at breakfast, lunch and supper times.

On the fifth or seventh day the initiands have their hands ceremonially washed or 'dipped' and from this time onwards they use them for eating (duly washing them again before each meal).

After the washing of hands itself many ceremonies occur, for the purpose of instruction. Their order and timing may not be the same in all instances of *tumdo* but the general pattern is similar.

When the hands have been 'washed' an arch is erected outside the circumcision lodge, in the middle of the pathway. Four sticks of *croton macrostachyus* species are tied together with a ritual creeper to form an arch about 4 feet high.[59] A stick for cleaning gourds is tied to each corner while bunches of stinging creeper and a hornets' nest are placed on the top.[60] Some cowdung is spread round the base and overlaid with fruit of the *solanum* plant and a little hole, dug in the centre under the arch, is filled with cow's urine. The initiands pass under the arch four times, each time putting the right foot in the urine. The warriors beat the hornets' nest, each time releasing hornets and pouring cow's urine over the bare bodies of the initiands. The urine, says one informant, is 'poured on top as a blessing to show appreciation for cattle'.

Every ordeal during *tumdo* is preceded and followed by the singing of special circumcision songs. Such songs precede the trials which follow.

A club is tied with a creeper round the waist of the initiand while he is still naked. Then he is given a bow and an arrow and told to go to the circumcision lodge. On the way he is met by a man who informs him that a wild animal lurks inside and he must shoot. As the initiand steps on a twig the man hiding inside with a shield and small bells jumps out trying to frighten him. If the initiand appears frightened and runs away it is said that he is cowardly — like a woman, without 'any blood of a man in him'.

'There is a certain plant (like the banana tree) and the boy must shoot at it to see if he is accurate with the bow. If he is not successful abusive language is used and it is said that the boy may not be successful with a woman. The boy goes into the tunnel [arch] once again but not through. Somebody leads him to the tunnel to see something nice. But as he goes in his face is stung with nettles and he comes out with his face swollen, and suffers, feeling bitter ... '[61]

Circumcision is over, the 'passing out' has begun. I have two slightly differing accounts of another ceremony performed at this time. I give these accounts *verbatim*:

The major ceremony consists of the 'removal of a clot from the urethra' that will complete the process of circumcision. An arrow — a stick with a yellow round fruit of a particular type, *labotwet* — is directed at the boy's penis.

A bent stick stuck to the ground and attached to a long wire is supposed to be introduced into the urethra to pull out the clot. The boy's eyes are covered.

Normally there is singing before and after the ceremony is done on each of the boys. The old man conducting this usually only touches the penis and pours cow's blood on the wire preferably with a clot in it. When the boy opens his eyes he is told [that] the clot came from his urethra — some blood having been poured onto the penis.[62]

Next day he [the initiand] is taken to a man who says, 'Look here, you think you have been circumcised, you have not. We want to remove all that dirt you had as a young boy'. So, in order to make the boy clean he hits the testicles for all the dirty things to come out. The boys feel bad at more hurt. 'Do you want to see it to show you're brave, or do you want to cover your face?' Some say 'Yes', others 'No'; but 'Yes' or 'No' the face is covered. Then somebody comes with a bow and a stick to represent an arrow. At the end of it is a yellow fruit (*solanum campylacanthum* sp.). The boy is hit four times to see if he gets frightened. Then it is said that a stick is put through the stomach to see if it is clean. Soil, *posho* and meat are put on the ground and are said to have come from the stomach. 'What have you been eating? Dirty inside.' 'Dirty' language is used to see if cowardly or annoyed.[63]

The instruction at the circumcision lodge during the seclusion after the washing of hands is carried out by young warriors, the sponsors and some elders. The initiands at this stage have their bodies smeared with white clay and are dressed in the long leather skirts worn by women between initiation and marriage and, when out hunting, wear hoods to cover their heads.[64] The age-mates and young warriors come and teach yet more special songs which, when mastered, are sung three times daily between meals.[65] The warriors also teach the initiands to make traditional weapons: spears, shields, bows, arrows, knives, clubs, walking sticks, etc. If they are not going to be presented by the elders with headdresses for coming out then the initiands also make headdresses during this time.

When sufficiently healed, the initiands go hunting in the daytime — never at night — making certain not to encounter women, not to cross farms, and not to cross roads or rivers without leaving the mark of a bow, a blade of grass or a leaf. If a woman is encountered inadvertently she is struck with a stick or shot with a wooden arrow. Nowadays, the initiands usually take three types of arrow on these hunting expeditions, one for killing snakes, one for killing birds and one for killing rabbits and dik-dik. The birds and animals are cleaned out and then left in the hot sun to dry. Gone are the days of big game hunting in Nandi, when buffalo, elephant, lion, leopard and antelope were common. This means that training and practice are minimal, completed in three weeks or even less, the more so when even cattle raiding is illegal! In the past, at least six months were spent hunting game and learning to raid cattle.

Sometimes the sponsors prolong their daily visit and stay to sleep. They give instruction in the identification and use of trees, shrubs and herbs used for medicinal and ritual purposes. They give detailed instructions in the ritual procedures of *tumdo*, particularly the building of the *kimusanyit* arch. The social organisation of the Nandi together with tribal taboos, war tactics, raiding and care of cattle are carefully explained. Particular attention is paid to bravery, the behaviour appropriate to a man as distinct from a child or a woman and the treatment which ought to be accorded wives and old people.

Among themselves the initiands are ordered according to age-set seniority and the anonymity of a transitional phase. The senior initiand, the 'firstborn', takes charge of the distribution of the food and, in the absence of the sponsor, sleeps in his more comfortable bed. In the event of the 'firstborn's' indisposition the junior initiand, the 'lastborn', takes over. No one is addressed by name but by 'initiand' or by a whistle.

Concerning the reduction of time in this period of seclusion one schoolboy commented: 'During my father's time, for he is a *Chuma* ... and he is thought to have been circumcised in the late 1940s they used to stay for about one year but the presence of European knowledge has reduced the time to at present one month.'

11. *The Frightening*[66]

As the period of seclusion draws to an end, probably about three days before the 'coming out', the young warriors take bull-roarers into the bush and, simulating the howls of wild animals, frighten the initiands. They then enter the circumcision lodge and start to break it to pieces, jumping up and down on the sticks and the thatch. However, the initiands, determined to save the centre pole, kneel down and hold on to it tightly. After this episode the initiands learn and practise the use of bull-roarers and begin the singing of the songs which will accompany the *suiyet* dance later. They also collect the dried animals and birds in readiness for 'coming out'.

12. *Immersion*

The central event of what is commonly called *kapkiyai* is the immersion of the initiands in water.[67] Shortly after the 'frightening' the sponsors and circumcised men build a dam about 5 feet deep in the river near the circumcision lodge. An arch made of sticks is then erected in the water and a fire lit about 30 yards away. It is very early in the morning, about 5 a.m., when the initiands arrive. A man stands guard to keep women, children and any unwanted people away. A naked man sits on the top of the arch to show the way and the initiands, in ritual order, also naked and holding on to each other, file in and out through the arch and around it, both four times. All the time they sing the special songs of initiation. When standing, the water reaches above their chests and if they find the ordeal too difficult to endure it is reckoned that some omissions have been made in their confessions. Afterwards, they warm themselves at the fire and drink tea sent by their mothers.

When adequately warmed they are taken to another little structure built of curved sticks plaited round with a ritual grass and having a small doorway.[68] Each initiand proceeds inside four times where, on each occasion, he is stung on the face with a stinging creeper. The purpose, I am told, is to make their eyes bloodshot and red, unlike a woman's. From here the initiands go once again to the circumcision lodge (even if it is already half-dismantled) where they rest and eat, ready for the afternoon.

In the afternoon, still dressed in women's attire but wearing a head-dress made of the leaves of the wild date palm or grasses and decorated with the dried animals and birds killed during the hunting,[69] the initiands go to the clearing where the dance was held and sing and dance the *suiyet* in front of the assembled elders, women and children, paying particular attention to their mothers. They are not, however, as yet recognisable. This state of semi-seclusion may last for one or more days compared with up to eight weeks in the past. Indeed, nowadays, it often lasts for one afternoon only, the next part of *tumdo* taking place on the same evening.

An interesting addition to the central event of 'immersion' is recorded from South Nandi and adds to our understanding of the events of the day when the initiands acquire the new names of adulthood, decided on by their respective families. It is a 'mock killing' ceremony and was described to me as follows:

A log of wood or banana stem is taken to a river which has been dammed — placed by the river. As each boy comes he is asked where he comes from and whose son he is. On answering, the log is hit, cries of 'bring water' are made and this poured on the log. This happens to everybody. At the end they go for swimming, so cleaning their bodies ready for the outside world … [70]

13. *The Tightening of the Thong*[71]

It is evening when the dance finishes and the initiands are taken by their sponsors to the house of *tumdo* for the 'tightening of the thong'. This is perhaps the most secret of all the events of the ritual sequence. In a manner of speaking the elders inspect the initiands to see whether or not they have been well taught during their period of seclusion. More objects are brought forward for identification, some ordeals are repeated, and where knowledge is thought to be deficient the lesson has to be learned again. All the procedures of *tumdo* are described in great detail. The ceremony gets its name from the word *rige*, meaning 'thong', nowadays a ligament from a cow. The thong is put round the little finger of the right hand and jerked tight. In this manner the oath is administered to all initiands. As the thong is jerked they promise to keep all the details of *tumdo* secret. The procedure is very painful and the pressure is relieved only when the initiands promise to take the oath or be cursed. The ceremony is probably only one of many components of *rikset* albeit the most important. Ever afterwards a traditionally initiated Nandi man greets not with the whole hand but with the little finger of the right hand.

Meanwhile, all the assembled elders have been drinking beer while with the approach of dawn the invited guests have been preparing to attend the *ng'etunot* feast. Just as the commencement of *tumdo* called for rejoicing — *siei*, the special rejoicing shown when people go to circumcision — so too its completion and the 'coming out' of the initiates as fully-fledged warriors calls for a feast!

14. *The Welcome Back*[72]

At this point in *tumdo* only the main happenings appear to be clearly defined. Due to the telescoping of events neither timing nor sequence appears to be uniform throughout Nandi nowadays. The reader must bear in mind therefore that the following account is but one (albeit the most common) ordering of the closing events of *tumdo*.[73]

The 'tightening of the thong' ceremony having finished at dawn, the initiands bathe in the river, dress in women's garments, put on the ritual headdress and prepare to re-enter society as fully-initiated men ready for war and marriage. Parents and guests attending the feast present them with gifts of clothes and money while mothers in particular greet them with the singing of the *torokset* — songs to greet those coming after a long absence. Then, wearing necklaces presented by the women, they visit in procession the houses round about. They spend the night with their sponsors and early the following morning go down to the river to bathe and don their new clothes — probably shorts or trousers and a shirt — after which they set out for their respective homes, being now known as 'initiates'.[74]

On arrival home they are met and greeted, not as might be expected, by their mothers (who have deliberately gone into hiding), but by a sister, aunt or other female relative appointed by the family for the purpose. This girl anoints the initiate with clarified butter and the two enter into a special lifelong relationship of *bamwai*. Ever afterwards this girl may be called on to perform special services for her particular *bamwai*. There is great rejoicing in the home, although at present not for a sustained period. Instead of going to the warriors' communal hut and thence on raiding expeditions the young warrior most likely returns to school or goes in search of further training and employment.[75]

NOTES

1   Victor Turner takes the concept of liminality and applies it to a much wider context than a single ritual, for example to millenarian movements. (*The Ritual Process*, London/Chicago, 1969, p. 112.) Aylward Shorter extends the application to society as a whole: 'Turner has introduced us to the concept of the "liminal" ritual which is a prolongation of the liminal phase in a *rite de passage*, through which individuals find strength to meet the demands of a complex and highly structured society. Liminal rituals characterize liminal periods of history when an old social order is passing away, and a new one has not yet clearly taken shape.' (*East African Societies*, London/Boston, 1974, p. 94.)

2 The four sub-sets (*mostinwek*, sing. *mat*, meaning 'fire of circumcision') were *chonginiek* (sing. *chonginiot*, meaning 'ostrich feather'), *kiptaru*, *chetagat* or *tetagat*, and *kiptoinik* (sing. *kiptoiyot*, meaning 'the bull calf'). They merged to three, viz. *chonginiek*, *tetagat* and *kiptoinik* and then into two, viz. *chonginiek* and *kiptoinik*, those of the *Sawe* set, for example, being referred to popularly in English as 'Big *Sawe*' and 'Little *Sawe*'.

3 Those circumcised together were said to belong to the same *mat* (literally, 'fire') signifying that they sat around the same circumcision fire.

4 For details see G.W.B. Huntingford, *The Nandi of Kenya*, p. 62 and my 'Ritual Change among the Nandi', pp. 158-9.

5 NDPR, Vol. I, entry for 21 June 1926 (DC/NDI/3/1), Kenya National Archives, Nairobi.

6 G.S. Snell, *Nandi Customary Law*, London, 1954, p. 99.

7 It was called *sagetab eito*, meaning literally 'the dividing of the white bullock', from *sach*, meaning 'to divide meat', 'to divine' and *eito*, meaning 'white bullock'. For details see A.C. Hollis, *The Nandi*, pp. 12-13 and G.W.B. Huntingford, *The Nandi of Kenya*, pp. 68-9, and also my 'Ritual Change among the Nandi', pp. 114-18.

8 The area was *bororiet*.

9 The platoon was *siritiet*, the commanders *kiptainik* and the senior sub-set *chonginiek*. For details see my 'Ritual Change among the Nandi', pp. 118-21.

10 Cf. N.Q. King, *Religions of Africa*, New York, 1970, p. 69.

11 The preparation is known as *sogotet* or *sogoteriot ab tumdo*, meaning literally 'preparing for the ceremony'.

12 Sponsors are *motirēnik* (sing. *motiriot*). The word has been variously translated 'tutor', 'specialist', 'guide', 'instructor', and 'godfather/godmother'. I have avoided the translation 'specialist' because the *motirēnik*, although specialists and experts at their job, do not belong to a special class in Nandi society. The 'master of ceremonies' is *boiyob tum*, meaning literally 'elder of the ceremony'.

13 If they belong to a more senior set it must not be the set of the initiands' fathers.

14 In the past, *tumdo* was a major event held at area level. There were many pairs of sponsors, each pair having up to ten boys in their care. At times, today, there may be up to ten boys circumcised together but it is not usual.

15 The Nandi fumigate their gourds with charcoal and clean them out with the dried centre rib of a palm-frond called *sosiot* (*phoenix reclinata* sp.). Prior to the coming of the Europeans it was taboo in Nandi to boil milk. Two milk drinks were made in the fumigated gourds, both with a charcoal flavour: fermented milk, with or without blood (called in Nandi *mursik*) and fresh milk. Nowadays, generally speaking, the former is not taken with blood.

16 The beer, *maiyek*, is stored in large earthenware pots called *terenik*; the stiff porridge is known as *kimnyet* and the gruel as *musarek*.

17 In Nandi *kiyokto komwaita tumdo*.

18 In Nandi *tekset nebo menjet*.

19 Apparently the hut may have two rooms, one for the initiands, the other for the sponsors.

20   In Nandi *tebeswet* (*croton macrostachyus* sp.).

21   The broad-bladed knife called in Swahili *panga* is a multi-purpose instrument in widespread use throughout East Africa.

22   I was given the terms *chebo* and *ne ming'in* for the senior and junior sponsors respectively.

23   The leader is called *kiboret*, literally 'firstborn' and the last *towet*, literally 'lastborn'.

24   From *aiywa*, meaning 'axe'.

25   The small gourd called *mwendet* has a hole in its side from which the elder expectorates.

26   The shrine, called in Nandi *korosiot*, is a structure made of ritual plants — *korosek* — about 2-3 yards from the back door of a Nandi house, to the east, or to the left as one enters. It is usually between 2 and 6 feet in height — I observed one about 4 feet — and is made by placing four (some say eight) sticks of ritual plants in a circle and binding them together with a rope of one of the ritual climbing plants. It is at *korosiot* that prayer to *Asis* is made before the performance of important ritual acts during initiation and marriage. Fire is present either beside it or in its centre. For a discussion of this subject and the root **koros* generally see my 'Ritual Change among the Nandi', pp. 342-54.

27   In Nandi *ngariet* and *tartariet* respectively.

28   The trees are *segetet* (probably *myrsine africana* sp.), *uswet* (*euclea schimperi* sp.) and *sugemeriet*.

29   The garment is called in Nandi *kiboet* and is a short calfskin, sheepskin or goatskin garment worn over the shoulder.

30   A.C. Hollis, op. cit., p. 53.

31   In Nandi *kabonyony*.

32   Wattle (*acacia mearnsii* sp. — black — and *acacia podalyriifolia* sp. — silver leaved, golden) was introduced into Nandi from Australia for economic reasons. The cassia is locally known as *senetwet*.

33   The 'curse', called in Nandi *chubisiet*, was believed to be effective.

34   In Nandi *cherset*, indicating songs and words of encouragement addressed to initiands during initiation.

35   In Nandi '*Korgotab oi!*'. The actual translation offered to me was 'You wife of the devil!', reflecting the Nandi Bible rendering of Satan or devil by '*Oi*', the Nandi word for 'ancestor' or 'shade'.

36   This is for three reasons at least: the language of the songs is archaic (often Maasai in origin) and veiled, while the content is esoteric by intent.

37   The nettle is called in Nandi *siwot*.

38   In Nandi *kailet*.

39   The ox-horn is called in Nandi *lalet*.

40   Some examples are as follows:

chemelet (a type of stinging creeper)   *moiyat* (a flowering shrub found in the valleys)

siwot (a nettle)	*ngwek* (vegetables)
tuga (cows)	*soenik* (buffaloes)
kwenik (firewood)	*itoik* (charcoal sticks for cleaning gourds) — *acacia* sp.
motiriot (sponsor)	*bamong'o* (father-in-law on husband's side or respected ancestor of the Nandi)

41 The poles are *mobet*, and the creeper *kimnyarindet* in Nandi.

42 The Nandi terms are *rigeito, sotet* and *twoliot* respectively.

43 The songs are known in Nandi as *keyang'nda* or *sinja*.

44 The Nandi are no great lovers of drums. Shields are often used as substitutes but during rituals the friction drum is employed. It is made by drawing a piece of goatskin taughtly over one end of a small wooden barrel or over the open neck of an earthenware water jar. An oiled stick is rested against the centre of the drum. A roaring noise is then produced when a man draws his hands up and down the stick in the manner of milking a cow. The noise resembles the roar of a wild animal.

45 In Nandi *chemuseriet*.

46 The knife is called *kibos* in Nandi.

47 A.C. Hollis gives a similar account of this part of the ceremony (op. cit., pp. 53-4).

48 In Nandi *muratanet*, from the verb *muratan*, 'to circumcise'.

49 In Nandi *tebeng'wet*.

50 The age-mates in 1972-3 belonged to the *Kipkoimet* age-set. If a spear is not used then the initiand is told to fix his gaze on a tree or bush about 50 yards away.

51 'Jimmy' Kimng'etich Arab Ketel is the son of a Nandi mother and a European father. At present he farms about 100 acres near the Catholic mission at Chepterit and lives on the plot where he was born. He also conducts business in Chepterit and Eldoret where he has business premises.

'Jimmy', as he is known all over Nandi, went to Nairobi in 1932 and was among the first medical assistants to be trained at the Medical Training Centre. He was baptized an Anglican in 1933, while in training. After the completion of his training in 1936 Jimmy was appointed to Kakamega in western Kenya where he remained for three years. From there he went to Kapsabet Hospital, to Nairobi for another two years and thence to Kabarnet in Tugen country for a few months. Afterwards he spent approximately twenty-five years at the Kapsabet Hospital until he retired in the 1960s.

Jimmy says that he began to circumcise Nandi boys in hospital 'about 1940'. He claims to be a Christian, asserting that he disapproves strongly of the full Nandi traditional circumcision rite for males. From then until now he has circumcised the children of Christians and Muslims. For the most part patients attended the hospital in the past while at present they visit him at home. For example, Reuben Seroney, first Anglican Vicar of Nandi, brought his son, Eric (now John and a politician), to be circumcised at the age of twenty. Only ten years ago Jimmy circumcised a group of ten Muslims at Tilalwa.

Jimmy's patients may or may not undergo the traditional rites in addition to the medical operation. He is often summoned to *tumdo* to perform the duty of a circumciser using injections and modern drugs; in other instances he is merely requested to buy modern drugs or medical aids, such as iodine, for the traditional circumcisers to use.

Another medical assistant, Daniel Sebulei of Kobujoi in South Nandi, operates along the same lines as Jimmy for his own area.

Jimmy has a large family and is married for a second time to a young Nandi woman. I interviewed him twice: on 16 October 1973 and again on 1 August 1974 and collected other people's opinions about him, also an assessment of his work. So many of the older people have such confidence in Jimmy as the 'curer of all ills' that they go to him in preference to the hospital. Officialdom is not too pleased, and in 1973 it was reported that he was fined 400 shillings for practising without a licence.

52 J.A.L. and M.K. (confidential).
53 J.A.L. and M.K. (confidential).
54 A.C. Hollis, op. cit., pp. 54-5. Two comments are in order here. On the whole, nowadays, the foreskins are not retained but placed first on the stool (without milk) and then dropped on the ground to be cleared away by the ants. Nowadays, the sponsors help the master of ceremonies administer the honey and water and perform the second and major stage of the operation.
55 If the circumcision lodge is a little distance from the clearing then great care is taken that the initiands are surrounded by persons covering them in leaves so that no female or uncircumcised male beholds them. Warriors accompanying the returning procession may chase the women away with sticks.
56 In Nandi *labet-ab-eun*, literally 'the stitching' or 'the sewing' of hands.
57 In the past, the period was much longer, about one month; even today some report a period of fourteen days between *muratanet* and *labet-ab-eun*.
58 Between the time of the operation and the 'coming out' all initiands are in a state of ritual uncleanness of the second degree — *kerek*. However, if misfortune befalls them, for example, if the circumcision lodge catches fire or they shout too loudly instead of speaking softly, then they are temporarily in a state of ritual uncleanness of the first degree. Cf. A.C. Hollis, op. cit., pp. 91-2, for a description of the three degrees of ritual uncleanness and the prescribed purification procedures.
59 The tree is *tebeswet*, and the creeper used is *sinendet* or another used in erecting *korosiot*.
60 The stinging creeper is called *chemelet*.
61 J.A.L. and M.K. (confidential).
62 H.N. (confidential).
63 J.A.L. and M.K. (confidential).
64 The skirt is called in Nandi *nyorgit*.
65 They are known in Nandi as *kaandaet*.
66 In Nandi *kamuiset*.
67 In Nandi *kapkiyai*, 'the place of immersion', more accurately *kayaiset*, describing the action.
68 The grass is *tebeng'wet, veronia auriculifera* sp.

Two informants insert another test at this point; they are probably quite correct in doing so as many such take place:

Then they are taken to another place. After the operation they are asked if they would like to sleep with a woman and they say 'No' as it would be very painful. Now they are told 'We've been always telling you that one day you would sleep with an old woman, now you'll know.' They are taken to a place where three images of clay representing woman, husband and child stand. 'See these people, this is the mother and this is the daughter, which do you want tonight?' The boys must answer,

'The girl'. But unless the girl is circumcised this is not good. 'You're now a man, an initiate, from today onwards we allow you to sleep with any man's woman. If you're found out it's dangerous, but if not then it's not bad. Here is the woman, have intercourse!' The boys pretend to have intercourse with the clay image. It is pronounced all right, they are overcoming. Again they go into the small hut where nettles are rubbed into the face until it is very red ... (J.A.L. and M.K. confidential.)

69 The headdress is called in Nandi *morongochet*.

70 H.N. (confidential). Normally, the name given is that of 'the son of' So-and-so — *Arap*. It is the father's 'porridge' or second name which is employed. For example, if his father's name is *Kipruto* (meaning 'born on a journey') he will be *Arap Ruto*. He could, however, be named differently, especially if a younger son.

71 In Nandi *rikset*, from the word *rige*, meaning 'thong'.

72 In Nandi *torokset*.

73 For instance, *rikset* may go on for more than one night, after which initiands may travel around the countryside for a week, before going home.

74 In Nandi *kipkeleloik*.

75 The *sigiroinet* was the warriors' communal hut where they could sleep with uncircumcised girls and in the past, at the conclusion of the *ng'etunot* feast, they lived there by themselves for a month.

V. Female Initiation

To 'come out' is by definition to 'make début on stage or in society'. Making use of the second of these two meanings we can say that *tumdo*, in the past, was a Nandi girl's 'coming out' ceremony. By putting their daughters through initiation Nandi parents declared their daughters' eligibility for marriage and their own readiness to receive suitors. This is still true today, but with some qualifications. Some girls get married nowadays without being circumcised, while others are circumcised on reaching the age of puberty without any immediate reference to marriage.

1. *Timing*

Until marriage a Nandi woman is classed as a 'girl' although she is known by distinct terms before circumcision and between circumcision and marriage.[1] After marriage she becomes in turn a 'married woman' and an 'old woman'.[2] Nandi women have no age-sets of their own but rather join their husbands' on marriage.

The first major factor in the timing of *tumdo* is the age-set system. In the past, it was the timing of the age-set system's major events which largely controlled the age at which girls were initiated. Consequently, changes which have affected the age-set system have also affected the timing of *tumdo*. They are somewhat as follows.

In days gone by, a boy's sex life began only after he had come out from initiation and then he might be as old as twenty-five. Furthermore, the form of intercourse sanctioned after initiation and before marriage was intercrural and a warrior did not normally marry until he had spent a few years in active service — fighting and raiding cattle. Nowadays, however, a boy is on average fifteen years old when initiated and from that moment onwards he is entitled to have sexual relationships with uncircumcised girls. Due to a decline in the use of the warriors' communal hut, today, it is more than likely that a young couple will meet in the boy's private living quarters and engage in full intercourse.[3] The implication of this for the timing of girls' circumcision festivals is a lowering of the average age at which Nandi girls marry, and, as we have seen, clitoridectomy normally precedes marriage. Some, already in the early stages of pregnancy, may wish to be circumcised in haste so as to become eligible for marriage as soon as possible. Others, having made their own choice of partner, may wish to elope and undergo clitoridectomy and marriage clandestinely without parental consent.

The second major factor affecting timing is education.[4] Today, girls wait until they have completed either primary or secondary schooling before going to *tumdo*. And, as we have seen, there is a growing number of girls not undergoing clitoridectomy at all.

The third major factor affecting timing is availability of food. Traditionally, *tumdo* took place if and when there were sufficient girls in a neighbourhood to make the holding of the event worthwhile. Numbers varied from neighbourhood to neighbourhood but usually five to ten girls were considered sufficient. The normal season in which the event took place was harvest time — from October to December or thereabouts, and there was no year when, in theory, clitoridectomy could not be performed. Today, harvest is still the most popular of seasons for *tumdo*, but I have known it to take place frequently in April and August. Availability of food all the year round is largely responsible for this latter innovation, and it has in time led to a reduction in the number of girls going through *tumdo* at any one time. Groups now average two to three girls. In addition, a considerable number are circumcised without any companions — pointing to an increase in individualism. Similarly, the period of seclusion after circumcision has been reduced from 6-12 months to 6-12 weeks, while it is not unknown for girls to be secluded for only two weeks and then married.

2. *Preparation*[5]

'When a few girls living in the same neighbourhood have reached a marriageable age, their fathers decide to arrange a circumcision festival', wrote A.C. Hollis in 1908.[6] Indicative of the arrival of the modern age is the fact that today a girl often approaches her parents asking for *tumdo*. The matter is then taken up with the neighbourhood elders and a date and place fixed. The elders may think it fitting to make extensive enquiries about the girl's character. Expectations are not, however, idealistic, it being considered more important that the girl is well-known in the neighbourhood. Perhaps a more important consideration, practically, is to ensure the availability of an adequate supply of food for feeding her while in seclusion. These matters in hand, the parents choose a 'mistress of ceremonies' and two 'sponsors'.[7] The former will organise the ritual procedure and the latter will act as tutors to the initiands for the duration of the ritual and subsequent period of seclusion. All three must be experts in matters of ritual.

Next in order of importance today is the acquisition of the ceremonial outfit. Tradition requires that the girl be clothed in full warrior's ceremonial dress, and today this dress is normally either hired or borrowed. Some women specialise in making these outfits now that the warriors' dress is very scarce and, in addition, provide when necessary the services of male experts to supervise the putting on of the attire — a part reserved in the past for the girl's 'sweetheart' from her days in the communal hut.

The outfit acquired, or at least its acquisition set in motion, the candidate for initiation takes a few girls junior to her in age — and likely soon to be initiated — and between them fix some thigh-bells just above their knees. They each take a whistle and any fly whisks which may be available and set out to tell relatives (particularly on the mother's side) and neighbourhood about *tumdo*. Often, they travel as far as 20 miles from home whistling and singing as they go. As they approach the household belonging to a relative they sing at first, this being considered sufficient indication of the purpose of the visit. The songs employed are carefully rehearsed every evening and are in the nature of folksongs, often in praise of important people, and intended for singing at the dance during the opening of *tumdo*. Invitations must be issued personally, and nowadays are often followed up by letters or formal invitation cards.[8] It is quite common during circumcision seasons in Nandi to meet such groups of girls skipping along the road, singing and whistling as they go. Then, in the evenings, as darkness approaches, sounds of whistles and song rend the air, along the hillsides and across the valleys, as the dance gets under way. For, in the evenings, during these weeks, until three days or so before *tumdo*, the girls are allowed to be with their boyfriends. Both days and evenings are used by the girls to practise the songs for *tumdo*.

Meanwhile, at home, the womenfolk sew garments, daub houses, and prepare food and drink.

Then, about three days before *tumdo*, the girls return home to rest and go to the shops. There they buy the various necessities for the modern *tumdo* festivities: soft drinks for all, cigarettes for the young men, sweets for the children, gifts of kitchen utensils or household requisites for close relatives and a new outfit — trousers, shirt, etc. — for the 'sweetheart'.[9] If western-style dancing is planned then a gramophone and records, or cassette player and tapes, are acquired, probably at a fee, and a marquee-like structure erected near the main houses being used for the activities. Father helps to brew the beer and kill the ox (if he is wealthy enough!). But if relatives from some distance have already arrived then a sheep or goat is slaughtered. Such is the mark of Nandi hospitality.

Even today, guests, women in particular, wear some vestiges of traditional dress — earrings, necklaces, bracelets, beaded belts and skin garments. Often, too, the women shave their hair from ear to ear.

3. *Shaving the Head*[10]

By the morning of the day when *tumdo* is due to begin — probably a Friday or Saturday — guests from afar will have arrived and been accommodated and fed. During the day, the womenfolk will assist relatives and neighbours in collecting firewood, fetching water and putting the finishing touches to the preparation of food, beer and honey-wine.

Top: 5. Announcing *tumdo. Above:* 6. Ritual fetching of firewood.
Below: 7. Preparing for *tumdo.*

Left: 8. Initiand in warriors' dress, *c.*1905.

Below: 9 and 10. Initiand in warriors' dress, 1973.

Opinions differ as to precisely when and where, but it is most likely in the morning at the shrine which has been erected by the back door of the mother's house (serving as the ceremonial house) that the candidate has her hair shaved by the sponsors.[11] It is thrown towards the east and prayers are offered to *Asis*. Normally, in the past, a purgative was administered at this point but the practice appears to have gone into decline. From this moment onwards the candidate is known in Nandi as *tarusiot*, a liminal person in a period of transition, although it appears to be more common at present to use this term after the physical operation of clitoridectomy. And even nowadays at this point she dons the traditional outer and also upper skin garments over her own clothes; the custom of smearing with fat and red ochre, however, has been abandoned.

On two occasions I personally witnessed initiands in ritual procession after lunch, at about 3 p.m. Led by their senior sponsor and followed by the junior sponsor they were returning from the forest where they had been collecting firewood. They were dressed in skin garments over their cotton dresses and had bells on their thighs, whistles round their necks and fly whisks in their hands. Sarah Cherotich has described and sought to interpret the collection of firewood in the following manner:

After this, the candidates, wearing their thigh bells, go to the forest to cut firewood with the help of other women and *motirēnik* who will help them through initiation. One teacher holds the axe and one girl comes forward and holds it too, then they both cut the wood. The other girls take their turns with this teacher. This having been done, they all go home, carrying the firewood to the house where the ceremony is being held. There is some kind of unity sought in this cutting of wood. The teachers want to show the girls that from now on they are united, and each girl is part of the others, not individuals ... [12]

Sometimes, I have been told, the examination of the initiands to determine whether or not they are virgins takes place at this point or even earlier. But so far as I can ascertain this examination takes place more commonly in the evening as soon as the singing and dancing have begun.

4. *Transvestiture*

About mid afternoon when the firewood has been collected, the initiand's 'sweetheart' arrives with his friends to dress his girl. They bring with them quantities of the *sinendet* plant, a ritually significant creeper, and often address the girl with words of encouragement such as 'Go very well', adding her name. The 'sweetheart' may be assisted by a man who has become professional at the job, for, in the modern *tumdo*, the transvestiture has assumed a prestigious position: it has become a significant focal point of social attention.

When, in December 1973, I attended *tumdo* at Sang'alo, the initiand's 'sweetheart' was away from home in the army and, incidentally, about to travel to Christchurch, New Zealand, to represent Kenya in the Commonwealth Games. Her brother, a schoolboy at Kapsabet School, took his place in the ceremony and also to him fell the responsibility of bearing the cost of the feast and other expenses incurred.

At the beginning of the century, warriors' dress, apart from arms, comprised arm bands, leglets and a single blanket. Nowadays, the outfit — in Nandi *karik* — comprises dress, headgear, footwear and ornaments of a very elaborate nature as follows:

— a warrior's 'kilt' in orange-coloured jinja cotton
— a man's shirt
— a man's tie
— an apron-piece of colobus monkey skin with mirror attached and tied round the waist at the back[13]
— leglets and epaulettes of colobus monkey skin
— many-coloured headsquares sewn on the two shirt sleeves
— white knee socks
— plimsolls, ankle-length and laced
— beaded belts
— warriors' thigh bells and possibly ankle-bells
— fly whisk made of horse hair and of Maasai origin if possible[14]
— whistle
— an ornamental version of a warrior's headdress.[15]

At about 7 p.m. on the Friday evening when I arrived for the *tumdo* festivities at Sang'alo the initiand's brother was putting the finishing touches to dressing her in lavish attire hired for the occasion. The only part of the dress not hired, and purchased respectively by the brother and some boy friends, were the necktie and shirt with headsquares attached. The necktie in particular has taken on symbolic significance, as it were. It must be bought new for every occasion of *tumdo* because, as the distinctive mark of a modern Nandi schoolboy, it represents the warrior's dress actually presented *in toto* by the 'sweetheart' in days gone by.

5. *The Dance*

When the initiand has been dressed she and her friends form a small circle and begin to sing and dance in an anti-clockwise direction. Some informants were insistent that this first dance takes place round the shrine. The songs and dances employed are those which have been practised for weeks. The dance movements are vigorous but uncomplicated, consisting largely of an up-and-down movement accompanied by a shaking of the buttocks. The initiand is very obviously the centre of attention and her little circle becomes enclosed by an outer circle of women shouting words of encouragement. The men linger at its periphery. If there are any young men about due to be circumcised in the near future she seeks them out sometime in the evening, calls them into the circle, and sings words of encouragement to them. The girls accompany their singing with shrill whistles, tinkling thigh-bells and swishing fly whisks. As the excitement mounts, 'warriors' jump high into the air, girls break down and sob, women shriek and scream loudly and members of both sexes reach pitches of hysteria often culminating in their falling to the ground faint and unconscious. The latter are, however, immediately attended to and given help to enable them to regain control of themselves. Undue display of emotion, genuine as against feigned hysteria and drunkenness are not easily condoned by the Nandi and on these occasions can be regarded as potential sources of embarrassment to visitors. Drunkenness issuing in quarrelsomeness and ribaldry is particularly disliked. In general, the Nandi are reticent about showing emotion.

Nowadays, as traditionally, the songs sing the praises of courageous, brave and popular people, together with warriors and leaders and those who have successfully undergone *tumdo*. They also extol the virtues of *tumdo* as an institution and other qualities generally approved in Nandi society, and lastly the initiand herself. The repertoire is usually limited. Some are newly composed, others handed down from a previous generation and yet others pertain to a particular district of Nandi. I have heard songs extolling *tumdo*, songs praising 'sweethearts' and songs singing the virtues of popular heroes and tribal and national leaders. The latter were in praise of Kipchoge Keino, the Nandi Olympic gold-medallist; John Seroney, Member of Parliament for the Tindiret area; and President Kenyatta of Kenya together with President Nyerere of Tanzania.[16]

I offer here some freely translated versions of a few of these songs.

1. *How do you do, girls?*
How do you do, girls? How do you do, girls?
How do you do, girls? Tomorrow we say goodbye.

This song is sung in order to enable the initiand to break with her former friends with whom she will not be free to associate any longer.

2. *Kipchoge the man who runs for Kenya*
Lalego lalego lalego lalego
See Kipchoge the man
Who runs for his country Kenya.
Kipchoge, the man Kipchoge,
He runs for Kenya ...
     [repeated continuously]

3. *Who will open the door for Manori?*

Who will open the door for Manori?
Who will open the door for Manori?
Elizabeth will open for Manori.

Manori the son of Cheruiyot,
He brings fire in his nose.[17]

Who will open the door for Manori?
Elizabeth will open for Manori.

Manori when he sleeps cannot be awakened,
And he will not be lifted up;
It is terrible,
If lifted up he can kill people,
It is terrible.

Who will open the door for Manori?
Elizabeth will open for Manori.

Manori the son of Birech's Cheruiyot,
He cannot be lifted up.

Who will open the door for Manori?
Elizabeth will open. Manori *lalego ho!*

Who will open the door for Manori?
Elizabeth will open, *Ya — haa — haa* Manori!

Elizabeth will open the door.

In this song Elizabeth is the initiand and Manori her 'sweetheart'.

4. *People of Kenyatta love the daughter of Nyerere*

People of Kenyatta love the daughter of Nyerere,
Dance *lalego, lalego ee,* dance.

The daughter of Nyerere is at home,
Dance *lalego, lalego ee,* dance.

People of Kenyatta love the daughter of Nyerere,
Dance *lalego, lalego ee,* dance ...
[repeated continuously]

I recorded other songs at Sang'alo: one ridicules the harshness of the young men and taunts them about taking advantage of the girls, saying 'I promise ... '; another extols the beauty of the initiand comparing her to the tall sweet sugar canes of Kampala and exhorting her to face clitoridectomy bravely.

After the first session of singing and dancing the girls often go indoors to have refreshments.

Obviously, minor details of ritual sequence vary from one performance of *tumdo* to another; I have found such differences to be of little consequence. When, however, setting side by side numerous accounts and comparing them with my own observation I found one major variation in the ritual sequence — the timing of the recognition of the initiand's virginity. But even that is more apparent than real. It seems best therefore that the account below follow the sequence which I observed at Sang'alo.

After refreshments, the group proceeds to the house set aside for *tumdo*. At Sang'alo, because there was only one candidate it was the initiand's mother's house; for the duration it was called the 'house of *tumdo*'. Then they sing and dance as before. The poise and confidence of the initiand become increasingly evident as she shows herself in control of the situation generally, pushing back children encroaching on the circle and dancing with greater ease and more vigour than her companions. Elderly women and children constitute the majority of onlookers as the men present begin to drift away. The elderly men take their drinking tubes to the beer drink and the young men proceed to a clearing where a large bonfire has been lit. There, they dance the special dance called *chepkongo* by forming a circle and moving round the fire in an anti-clockwise direction, each with his hands on the shoulders of the man in front.

Next, the mistress of ceremonies and the two sponsors arrive and take the initiand into the house of *tumdo*. There, she is given instruction and advice about her behaviour during the operation and afterwards. She is also examined as to suitability of character. Most likely, too, at this time, the examination to test the girl's virginity takes place. Her legs apart, the initiand's vagina is closely examined by the sponsors. They peer and explore until satisfied as to the girl's condition. She, of course, if unjustly accused, will protest vehemently. For virginity is a virtue to be rewarded with gifts and many favours, the more so today as the vast majority of girls conceive before marriage. The virgin receives not only a place of honour during the operation but special recognition on coming out of seclusion and during nuptials.

One of my informants provided me with an interesting description of the girl's entry into the house of *tumdo* for this examination. It parallels the initiation ordeals administered to boys and has the ring of authenticity. Naturally, old women were reluctant to speak about such matters; it appeared to come much more easily to the menfolk to relate details of a sexual nature:

During the night of this dance, the candidates are taken to a house. In the house, a woman is seated in the loft, where firewood is usually stored. She sits there exposing her private parts, i.e. the vagina. When the candidates enter the house they are asked what the exposure is. When they answer the usual name they are told that that is not the answer. They are told that it is known as '*ngenda*' which literally means a kind of soil eaten by cattle.

After examination, if declared suitable, the initiand emerges from the house of *tumdo* garlanded in the *sinendet* creeper. Then, after a little more dancing outside the house, the party, followed this time by women and children only, proceeds to the paternal uncle's house.[18]

At first they sing and dance but then they stop to sing *kipsegoit*. This is a song of encouragement to the initiand and for women only. Paradoxically, men do listen. It often tells the girl that soon she will be no longer a girl but a woman bearing children. As the initiand stands by the door flanked on either side by a sponsor the women begin to chant softly and a soloist strikes up the main song above the rest. The person to begin is usually an elderly woman specially close to the initiand concerned on her mother's side. Next, the girls take the lead and finally the initiand herself. Meanwhile all the women are chanting softly after which they join in the singing and finally conclude in a rising crescendo. I recorded some parts of the *kipsegoit* at Sang'alo and following is the English translation:

```
A — aa — aa — _____Ha — oo — oh ⎫
A — aa — aa — _____Ha — oo — oh ⎪ all
A — aa — aa — _____Ha — oo — oh ⎬ together
A — aa — aa — _____Ha — oo — oh ⎭
```

Go to circumcision successfully, Chelimo!
Go to circumcision successfully, Chelimo!
Go to circumcision successfully, daughter of Maasai!
Go to circumcision successfully, nothing will happen!
Go to circumcision successfully, our mother,
  nothing will happen!

Some informants say that *kipsegoit* is sung first at the house of the circumciser who leads in singing the solo part. Traditionally, this would have been the house of the mistress of ceremonies who held the only office of leadership open to women in Nandi.

At Sang'alo *kipsegoit* was repeated at the grandmother's house and again outside the mother's. Then, the men started to return, probably in anticipation of the next public event of the ritual. Also at this juncture, a woman became hysterical and the uncle came to the rescue aided by the older women.

Kipsegoit over, the initiand goes into the house of *tumdo* for further instruction and advice. As time is getting on the sponsors pull her clitoris vigorously and apply nettles.[19] It is the custom in some parts of Nandi, in addition, to tie the clitoris tightly with a tendon in order to prevent the flow of blood, induce swelling and reduce pain later. But sometimes, neither nettle nor tendon is employed. Consequently, during the operation the girl's labia as well as her clitoris can get mutilated.

The ordeal over, the initiand and her companions proceed to the clearing and dance until midnight near the bonfire. At the same time the young men sing and dance, joking and jumping into the air.

Meanwhile, those of us at Sang'alo witnessed an extraordinary and interesting event. One of the initiand's companions had suddenly become so anxious to be circumcised that without any prior warning or preparation she entered the house of *tumdo*. By her action she put the women in charge under an obligation to circumcise her. A schoolgirl, newly-arrived from neighbouring Eldoret to join her friend's activities, she caused her parents considerable anguish. On reflection, however, (or so I am told) the father at least became reconciled to the fact, as his daughter's precipitate action had done him a favour by saving him the expense involved in laying on festivities for *tumdo*. As for the girl herself, she was so overwhelmed by the psychological and emotional effects of her action that she didn't appear among the company for the rest of the evening.

The next part of *tumdo* is one which many of the young men have been eagerly awaiting: at about midnight cigarettes and sweets are fetched. By the light of the bonfire the initiand casts her eyes around, searching for friends and relatives. She enquires after any who are not conspicuous and appears distressed if any are absent from this momentous event in her life. Then she gives cigarettes to her helpers for lighting and distributes them to her boy friends. Nevertheless, nowadays, many who are neither friend nor relative get some of the spoils. Similarly, sweets are passed round to the children but even old men and visitors get their share. Sometimes, too, the adults receive soft drinks. For a short time afterwards some of the young men continue to sing and dance while others turn homewards as soon as they have received their presents.

6. *Encouragement*[20]

The encouragement is the climax of the day's events. All the varied proceedings of the evening have been building up to this most solemn occasion, called in Nandi *cherset*.

A large circle is formed round the fire, men on the inside and women on the outside. At one side facing east stands the initiand with one sponsor on her right, the other on her left. Immediately opposite them, facing west an elder, close relatives and other men line up according to age-set rank. The elder then bids all present kneel. Men remove their hats and if perchance they have been chewing tobacco take it out of their mouths. At Sang'alo, this was the only point when it appeared to us that a lack of organisation prevailed. The older men of the 'senior elder' generation and the younger men of the 'warrior' generation argued at length as to which direction they should face, while the rest struggled with kneeling on the damp grass![21] Eventually, the dispute settled, the elder — at Sang'alo a close paternal relative of the initiand — rose to address the assembled company thus:[22]

ELDER: All these people in the company, listen!
PEOPLE: We listen.

ELDER: This ceremony is good, say good!
PEOPLE: Good.

ELDER: Let everybody give birth, birth, say give birth!
PEOPLE: Give birth.
ELDER: The bull and heifer give birth, say give birth!
PEOPLE: Give birth.
ELDER: They give birth to many, many, say many!
PEOPLE: Many.
ELDER: It is good, say good, it sounds like thunder, say thunder!
PEOPLE: Thunder.
ELDER: The bull and heifer, they are good, say good!
PEOPLE: Good.

He went on to address the initiand specifically and very directly, concerning her sexual relations. 'Have you ever gone to a cottage and refused to play sex with your sweetheart?', he enquired. The initiand's reply was intended to let the company know whether or not she was a virgin. If she were found to be so then it was the custom (and in some places still is) for her father to wear a special headdress from this time onwards.[23] Nowadays, he often dons it next morning after the operation or not at all.

The actual encouragement begins with the people still kneeling. First, an elder, the 'sweetheart', father and others in descending rank according to their age-sets take their knobkerries and walking sticks and stand directly in front of the initiand. Each in turn stretches his stick out over the girl's head and makes a speech. He praises, he cajoles, he mocks, scalds and rails, all with the purpose of steeling the nerves of the initiand to face the ordeal ahead. If she attempts to reach out for the stick, he withdraws it saying 'Do not think this is your mother's cooking stick or firewood ... ' She stands poised and confident and answers by dancing on the spot, blowing her whistle, shaking her thigh-bells and twirling her fly whisk. Eventually, the sponsors take the stick and place it by their side. At Sang'alo, knobkerries and walking sticks were in such short supply that the sponsors had to part with them repeatedly for further use. Now, the expectation of drama was so great that the initiand's brother acting out his role as 'sweetheart' feigned fainting with emotion, whereupon he was immediately lifted to his feet and led away.

I recorded some of the speeches which were often accompanied by promises of rewards for bravery. Following are a few of them, freely translated:

1. *'Don't be afraid!'*
I went to circumcision with your father,
I went to circumcision with your father;
And there was nothing that went wrong.

2. *'Look after your outfit!'*
Keep all these ornaments in a safe place
    when I go to sleep.

3. *'I've gone to great trouble to come'*

You go to circumcision tomorrow, it is no joke. I came by car, you don't know how much money I spent. I have a few things to tell you. Catch this stick of mine. I had it in hiding but I have removed it today.

All, it will be noted, have the intention of encouraging the initiand to be brave.

The encouragement concludes with a short prayer for a successful operation. The form is the same but word content differs from *tumdo* to *tumdo*. In one area the prayer is for deftness of touch (literally, 'hands that are *wisis*', *wisis* meaning 'easy', 'light') and the people respond 'light'. At Sang'alo, it was brief, concise and meaningful, a fitting conclusion to a serious ritual event:

ELDER: Blessed, say blessed!
PEOPLE: Blessed.

ELDER: Let the ceremony be successful, say successful!
PEOPLE: Successful.

ELDER: Let the circumciser (literally, 'sponsor') be quick, say quick!
PEOPLE: Quick.

ELDER: Rejoice, say rejoice!
PEOPLE: Rejoice.

ELDER: All people stand, say stand!
PEOPLE: Yes, stand.
(*Àa — ah king.*)[24]

After this, the crowd disperses, the majority to go home to their beds. The older men and some women, however, may spend the night around the beer-pot sipping and singing. Meanwhile, the sponsors take the initiand to the house of *tumdo*. There, the girl receives further advice and has more nettles applied to her breasts and clitoris.[25] She may get a few hours of sleep — it is by this time about 2 a.m. — sitting in a chair until daybreak.

7. *The 'Farewell' Breakfast*

Morning breaks to a flurry of preparation and excitement. While chairs and tables are set in readiness and refreshments fetched and spread, the initiand and her friends repeat some of the songs and dances of the night before. Breakfast soon follows.

At Sang'alo, on the suggestion of our hosts, we were awakened from our sleep (in the car parked nearby) at about 7 a.m. On arrival at the scene of the previous night's activities we saw for the first time since early the previous evening the girl who had impulsively offered herself for clitoridectomy without prior arrangement. As they danced, sang and mixed with the crowd the two initiands appeared in sharp contrast. One, mistress of the occasion, focal point of attention on this 'her day', was full of dignity. Exuding poise and confidence and showing no personal discomfiture after the ordeals of the night before, she acted the perfect hostess with ease and composure. The other, victim of an emotionally-charged drama, and feeling extremely sorry for herself, was sullen. Eyes brimming with tears she kept out of the public eye as much as she dared.

Very soon the guests begin to arrive, and this time they include many girl-friends of the initiands as well as young men and women carrying babies on their backs. Breakfast is served: tea and buttered bread, or soft drinks for those who prefer them. Meanwhile, the young people engage in western-style dancing in the marquee to the strains of music played on record-player or cassette recorder.

Breakfast over, dancing is suspended. A table, laden with gifts intended for relatives and friends, is placed before the initiand. Surveying hurricane lamps, glasses, enamel teapots, jugs, basins, mugs and plates she decides who will get what and then proceeds to distribute the gifts. The highlight is the presentation to her 'sweet-heart' of a 'box' or suitcase full of clothing and utensils, made either at this point or shortly afterwards at the shrine. At Sang'alo, of course, it was actually the initiand's brother who accepted the 'box' on behalf of her 'sweetheart'. Finally, the farewell is continued when the initiand sets out with her friends for quick visits to nearby houses and the local trading centre. There, she may solicit and receive gifts of money to help defray the expenses of *tumdo*. [26]

8. *The 'Anointing'*

The opening part of this part of the ritual is secret. Women elders prepare a fire by the shrine and take coals from it later to the centre of the circumcision circle. Then follows the ceremonial which bestows recognition and honour on virgins. A ceremonial Nandi stool, normally studded with beads, is brought into the centre of a circle formed round the shrine by a band of circumcised women. The initiand's father takes milk from a gourd and pours it into the depression on top of the stool. If she is a virgin the initiand swirls the milk with a fly whisk made from a cow's tail onto her father and other relatives standing nearby. She insists on not sitting down until her father promises her a pleasing reward for her honourable behaviour. In the past, a cow or even several cows were the norm, nowadays, money is most desirable and girls often repeat rhymes to the effect that they do not want cows as they have no plots of ground on which to graze them. Then the girl sits while the elders come to see her and relatives and friends shower upon her rewards in honour of her virginity.

There is some indication that sometimes this part of the ceremony takes place simultaneously with the 'encouragement' and includes questions relating to the subjects of sex, stealing and good relations — all important cultural themes of the Nandi.

Above: 11. Study in contrasts (the prepared and the unprepared). *Below:* 12. Singing and dancing.

14. After the 'anointing' at the shrine.

13. Choosing the gifts.

Following this, the father, maternal uncle, grandfathers and other close and elderly male relatives anoint the girls with clarified butter, or as it is known colloquially 'oil from the teats of a cow', from a small decorated ritual ox-horn. (At Sang'alo I observed the modern version: a small glass bottle with a rag stopper.) Finally, encircled by a number of elderly women with sticks resting on their shoulders, the initiand is led by her sponsors in ritual procession singing and dancing around the shrine. Meanwhile, the band of circumcised women are forming a circle in the clearing where the 'warriors' danced on the previous night while continuously singing songs such as this:[27]

> We shall get hold of Elizabeth today!
> We'll get hold! We'll get hold!
> We shall get hold of her when all are watching!
> We'll get hold! We'll get hold!

They stop when they see the initiand singing her final good-bye and throwing a calfskin, sheepskin or goatskin to her father, run towards the circle. As she does so they sing invitingly:

> *Oh — e — oiye leiyo*
> Come Elizabeth
> *Ee oiye leiyo ee o*
> *Ee — ee — mm — ei — mm*
> *Ei mm* — come Elizabeth.

and gradually enclose her in their circle.

The men, uncircumcised women and children are dismissed to a distance of 50 yards away or more. It is usually between 10 a.m. and 12 noon by this time.

9. *Clitoridectomy*

The mistress of ceremonies and the two sponsors receive the initiand into the circle. The colloquial term for this part of the ceremony is *tetwa*, meaning 'in order' and presumably referring to the setting of the initiands in ritual order and the formation of the women in a circle, ready for the operation.[28] When there are several initiands they are placed in ritual order according to virginal status and age-set seniority of their respective fathers. For the operation itself the stool of honour may be used to seat virgins while the rest of the initiands sit on skins spread on the grass. All sit with legs apart, held from behind by one sponsor and operated on by the mistress of ceremonies or the other sponsor. Holding the clitoris between the thumb and first and second fingers of the left hand the circumciser quickly cuts it with a small sharp knife called *mwatindet* or *mwaiteiyot*. It is intended that the clitoris only should be cut, but if anything goes wrong — insufficient preparation, a slipping of the operator's hand — then the labia can be

mutilated. Profuse bleeding may then ensue and girls have been
known to die even in recent years. Nonetheless, the Nandi rite, traditionally, is clitoridectomy and when performed correctly it is, from the
medical standpoint, not at all harmful.[29] After the cutting the
wound is dabbed with an application of ground millet meal dried on
the loft above the fire, but iodine and modern drugs are quite
commonly applied nowadays.

Only circumcised women and men who have lost brothers or
sisters in quick succession attend this part of the ritual. The women,
forming the circle, chant songs of encouragement, for example

Ari — ri — ri — ri — go well daughter!

while the girl's mother may run round the outer edges of the circle
crying and screaming in a distraught manner. If the initiand is brave
and courageous she is cheered and praised by the onlookers:

Ari — ri — ri — ri — thank you daughter of So-and-so!

Mothers and other female relatives take their big bunches of the ritual
climbing plant and run to their menfolk. They jump into their arms
with great excitement and elation and afterwards throw the garlands of
creeper about their necks. At Sang'alo I was able to take a photograph
of the uncle (standing in for the initiand's father) with the animal skin
over his shoulder, being greeted by the initiand's mother. For once,
great emotion is shown by a people usually undemonstrative and
reticent. The bunches of the ritual climbing plant used in the
ceremony are taken home by the relatives and friends and placed
triumphantly on the rooftops where they proclaim to all the completion of a successful operation. We too were garlanded, perhaps
because we were special guests.

If, however, the initiand shows any sign of cowardice or breaking
down it is considered very shameful. She is dubbed 'coward', in Nandi
chebitet, and must never attend another celebration of *tumdo*.[30]
She may also be put to a severe test, beaten by women in the circle,
and despised by those who have been brave. Relatives of an initiand
who has been dubbed 'coward' will go home shamefacedly without
saying farewell. Her 'sweetheart' will be almost inconsolate begging a
kind friend to spear him to death!

After the operation the initiand has her 'kilt' removed and replaced
by skins. Her 'sweetheart' receives back the warrior's regalia and nowadays returns individual items to owners from whom they have been
either hired or borrowed for the occasion. The initiand is kept hidden
from the eyes of outsiders, particularly men, and taken by the women
to her mother's or grandmother's house, where she will remain in
seclusion. Meanwhile, the sponsors are quick to administer medicine,
and give her milk to drink and gruel to eat if required.

Relatives and invited guests stay to lunch, while the old people resume their beer-drinking and the general public disperse and make their way home. At Sang'alo, we were considered to be invited guests and, garlanded with creeper, we were entertained to a large meal of meat, rice and maize porridge.

10. *Betrothal* [31]

Traditionally, the initiand's betrothal took place within three days of the operation. Normally, today, it does not take place until after the girl's 'coming out' of seclusion or even several years later, that is if it has not already taken place by mutual agreement of boy and girl. As, however, this is the proper place for betrothal in the ritual sequence I shall recount the details here.

'When a man is old enough he is to inform his parents about marrying his girl-friend', so writes a modern Nandi schoolgirl concerning the young man's role in the choice of a marriage partner. The matter is not so simple, however, and never has been although, according to Nandi tradition, a young couple intending to marry had some say in the matter. At the very least, their co-operation was sought and tacit recognition accorded to elopement. It is the custom for the parents of a girl of marriageable age to await approaches concerning marriage by the family of a suitable young man. [32]

Very early in the morning, at the waxing of the moon, one to three days following *tumdo*, hopeful parents set out with an engagement party for the initiand's home. The journey is known as *koito*. They take with them ritual plants. Each person has two sprigs of *cassia didymobotrya* species when available or in its absence leaves of the *solanum campylacantha* species. [33] On the way, members of the party watch and listen for a bird of omen. If it cries on the right the prospects are known to be poor, if on the left the party goes ahead in confidence and with great expectations. If it cries in front the way is being blocked, if behind it is calling for their return and so they must go home.

Meanwhile, at the initiand's home, the family is in all likelihood expecting engagement parties. In anticipation, the women of the house rise early, let out the calves, sheep and goats from the animal quarters of the house and get the room ready for the reception of visitors. [34] The bride-to-be remains in her small cubicle called *sumut*.

As the parties of suitors arrive, they pause at the back door by the shrine — if it is still standing after *tumdo*. The man who is to lead the negotiations (the suitor's father or paternal uncle) makes a special noise, as if to clear his throat, whereupon the woman of the house calls her husband and he receives the visitors. Unless the girl's family's relatives, however, are present to negotiate the bridewealth all suitors are dismissed and told when to return.

On the second visit, the initial proceedings are along the same lines as the first. Each party enters the animal quarters, presents the ritual plants and takes a position inside the door to the left, either kneeling or on haunches. 'Who are you?' asks the girl's family, meaning to what clan or sub-division of a clan does the family belong. Every kind of information is sought concerning the family, whether or not they are wealthy enough to afford a good bridewealth, whether or not any of its members have been found guilty of murder, theft or witchcraft, whether or not the family has a history of disease, malady or infertility. General investigations over particulars are discussed. Have the families had marriage alliances in the past? If so, it is asked whether the unions were fruitful or unfruitful. If the latter, then unless the elders reckon on a change for the better and give special sanction further inter-marriage cannot be considered. Of course the suitor's family will be equally concerned and will probably have gone into many of the questions before embarking on the journey in the first place.

Not more than two or three families and possibly only one will meet all requirements and they are told to leave the ritual plants inside the house. The rest are politely told to take their ritual plants and return home where they will be informed as to the date on which to return! The families or family chosen are then given back their ritual plants and told the day on which to return for final negotiations, probably the following day, when the suitor must be present in person.

A variant of this procedure is that when families know each other well and want their children to marry in order to strengthen the bonds of friendship they make enquiries behind the scenes and telescope the events. Educated and Christian families almost invariably do this.

In between the visits enquiries are continually being made as to the general character and suitability of the young people themselves. One of the main requirements is ability to work hard, as one Nandi saying has it: 'If a woman can do womanly jobs, she can qualify for marriage regardless of her beauty.'

On the third visit, after some further discussion as to character and bridewealth, one family remains. It is now the girl's opportunity to make her feelings known. She is asked if she agrees to the marriage proposal. Usually she concurs, although sometimes with reluctance, only assenting after some pressure from her parents. On other occasions, she refuses outright, whereupon she may be physically forced to agree if she does not manage to elope with her chosen lover.

When the actual amount of the bridewealth has been discussed and the engagement agreed to by all, the ceremony called *ratet* is embarked upon. From the verb *rat*, meaning 'to fasten', 'to tie', 'to bind', it has the metaphorical meaning of 'agreement', and comes close in meaning to the English 'betrothal'. The girl produces the small decorated ritual ox-horn called *lalet*, filled with clarified butter, provided either by the suitor's family or purchased with 20 shillings

15. Rejoicing after a successful operation.

16. The beer-drink.

17. Bridewealth certificate in AIC Records, Kapsabet.

given by them for the purpose. The fat is distributed with a cleaning-stick used for gourds and the relatives of the girl anoint in turn the relatives of the suitor: father anoints father, mother mother and so on. The fat is rubbed between the palms, spat upon in blessing, and smeared on head, arms and thighs of all concerned. Only the relatives on the suitor's side are anointed. Thenceforth, both parties to the anointing are known to one another as *bamwai*, denoting the existence of a special relationship authorising the mutual use of relationship terms as forms of address.

Furthermore, if there is any fear that the girl may be given to someone else, sponsors on the man's side bring long strands of *segutiet* grass, of the species *sporobulus* or *veronia*, oil them, spit on them, and place them on the right and left wrists of the boy and girl respectively. A song may then be sung while the ritual beer-pot in the centre of the room is being encircled. Then the strands of grass are removed at once, plaited and placed in the ritual ox-horn; alterna-tively some of them may be placed in a hole near the beer-pot, to remain buried. The grass in the ox-horn is taken by the parents of the suitor and guarded until the wedding day by his mother or sister. Despite all this, parents do marry their daughters to others. When this happens and no children result from the union, the parents of the dis-appointed suitor are entitled to produce the ox-horn containing the grass, summon the elders, have them spit on the girl, declare the second betrothal and marriage null and void and make the way ready for a reconciliation. The grass is then taken from the ox-horn and the girl 'given back' to the original suitor.

There is good reason to believe that such breaches of promise do happen, often with the sanction of both parents and elders, but under no circumstances are they considered honourable.

The betrothal ceremony over, the newly-related families drink specially-prepared beer and eat millet together, a ritual act of oneness in friendship and fellowship. And as the suitor and relatives journey home they anticipate the reception as the people enquire 'Have you been oiled?' or observe excitedly 'They have been oiled'.

One of two things follows on from the betrothal. Either the girl's intended husband visits her with gifts of food and oil for her head and body, providing her with a milch cow for the duration of her stay in seclusion or else he takes her to his parents' home where she is fed until her 'coming out' as a young woman ready for marriage. Whichever is the case he will not see her during the period of betrothal unless he steals a look at her face by removing her hood.[35] To make her pregnant at this stage would incur great shame. The former is more likely: the initiand stays at home awaiting her marriage and being looked after by her own family. On the rooftop is a sprig of the *cassia didymobotrya* species declaring to all and sundry that a member of the family has been betrothed.

11. *The Washing of Hands*[36]

As observed, betrothal does not normally take place within three days of the operation and I now resume where we broke off.

After the operation the newly-initiated girl goes into seclusion in a small compartment constructed with ritual plants inside the animal quarters of either her mother's or grandmother's house. She is in a state of uncleanness and traditionally was forbidden to touch food with her hands; instead she partook of it with a half-calabash. The sponsors look after her, feeding her with good food so that she gets fattened for marriage. On the fourth or seventh day the 'washing of hands' takes place. Hands are ceremonially washed or 'dipped' and thenceforth may be used for eating with. Knives, forks and metal spoons are used nowadays as well as or in place of the traditional wooden spoon or half-calabash. Thereby one degree of uncleanness is removed and the initiand may be visited by uncircumcised girls and children. No male visitors are allowed.

Clad in the long leather skirts of an older woman and heads hooded, some initiands are allowed to move around the surrounding district but only during the early hours of the morning or towards evening; others are kept in total privacy during their period of seclusion. If they wish to go outside during the daytime a small enclosure is erected outside the back door with sticks of the castor-oil plant. There the girls sit and sun themselves, their bodies smeared with castor-oil and ochre. Three times a day they join in special songs in praise of circumcision and those who bravely endured its ordeals, married women often accompanying them.

The seclusion period nowadays is a curtailed affair of two to twelve weeks. The norm is about five to six weeks if held during the school vacations. Elizabeth at Sang'alo was nineteen years old, circumcised in December and engaged to be married twelve weeks later in March-April. She had never been to school, yet was remarkably westernised.

During the seclusion period a girl is taught by her sponsors how to be a mature woman, a responsible person, a respectful wife and a good mother.

12. *The Frightening*[37]

When the end of a girl's period of seclusion is drawing near, 'warriors' come during the night, sound bull-roarers and frighten the initiand as she sleeps. It is intended as a trial of endurance and stress and as preparation for intensive instruction to follow.

13. *Immersion*[38]

Shortly after the frightening the initiand is led, early in the morning, to where a dam has been built in the river. There, led by her sponsors, she processes naked four times through an archway constructed in the deep pool. There, too, she is given a new name to befit her new status as a woman.

14. *The Tightening of the Thong*[39]

After the immersion and before her seclusion ends the initiand's relatives and guests arrive from near and far for a feast. As it progresses the initiand is examined as to whether or not she has been well-instructed and given further training where it is felt to be needed. Her little finger is tied and the thong pulled tight 'to help her not to forget that she has been sworn to secrecy'.

15. *The Uncovering*[40]

On the morning following the tightening of the thong the initiand is led by her sponsors to the river where she is washed and clothed in a married woman's attire, often nowadays a simple cotton dress. On arrival back at her mother's house she is met by her brother who 'unveils' (literally, 'uncovers') her publicly and anoints her with clarified butter. Thus is formed a special relationship between the two — henceforth they may address one another as *bamwai*. No longer a girl but a woman the newly-initiated may now wear a special headdress with a little bell suspended at its base and hanging along the nape of her neck. If a virgin she will also wear a pair of tusks protruding like horns above her forehead.[41] Thereafter, until married, she is known as an unmarried woman — *kipkileldet*. She has made her début, she has come out.

A newly-initiated young woman not due to be married immediately goes to stay with her mother and helps with domestic affairs while awaiting suitors to ask her hand in marriage. But she may, and nowadays often does, return to school, not to be married for years to come.

NOTES

1 *Chepto* is the general term for 'girl' but a girl is known as *somnyot* before clitoridectomy and *chepkileldet* or *kipkeleldet* between clitoridectomy and marriage.
2 *Osotiot* and *chebioset* respectively.
3 The *sigiroinet* was the unmarried warriors' communal hut where they could sleep with uncircumcised girls.
4 According to the 1969 census 46% of persons between the ages of ten and twenty-four years residing in Nandi District had undergone some form of schooling. Since then the first four years of primary education has been

made free. We can therefore expect this factor to become increasingly important. In June 1973 I administered an anonymous questionnaire in certain secondary schools in and around Nandi. Of 378 Kalenjin girls in secondary school (377 being unmarried) 330 (or 87.96%) had not been circumcised. Of the 176 who were Nandi 157 (or 89.72%) had not been circumcised. However, among their parents in the 35-45 years category 93.85% of both Kalenjin and Nandi women had been circumcised. For further details see my 'Ritual Change among the Nandi', p. 199.

5   The Nandi term is *sogotet*.

6   A.C. Hollis, *The Nandi*, p. 57.

7   The Nandi terms are *korgob tum* and *motiriot* respectively.

8   While interviewing a girl in Pokot (one of the Kalenjin sub-groups) I was informed of the circumcision party given by the District Commissioner for his daughter. It was no less than a cocktail party! Afterwards, while talking to one of the missionaries I ascertained that it was indeed the party which the missionary doctor and his wife had attended together with the VIPs of the area. We were in turn amazed and amused wondering if he were aware of the event's significance.

9   The 'sweetheart' of the *sigiroinet* was called *sandet*. Nowadays, his place may be taken by the initiand's brother or her fiancé or 'boyfriend', called *chemanet* (literally, 'lover'). I shall employ the word 'sweetheart' throughout.

10   In Nandi *konemunet ab metowek*, literally, 'the shaving of heads'.

11   The shrine, called in Nandi *korosiot*, is a structure made of ritual plants. For details see p. 42 n26 above.

12   Sarah Cherotich, 'The Nandi Female Initiation and Marriage and Christian Impact upon It', in *Dini na Mila*, Vol. II, No. 2/3, December 1967, p. 64.

13   In Nandi *koroiset*, in Kipsigis *ng'oisit*.

14   In Nandi *ng'otiot*.

15   In Nandi *kulo*.

16   The family of the initiand at Sang'alo had migratory connections with Tanzania.

17   Signifying 'one who comes with great strength and is harsh'.

18   This is the sequence of the Sang'alo occasion when the girl's uncle was standing in for her father.

19   Of the *siwot* variety.

20   In Nandi *cherset*, indicating songs and words of encouragement addressed to initiands during initiation.

21   In 1973 the young boys belonged to the *Kaplelach* age-set, the initiands to *Kipkoimet*, the warriors to *Sawe*, the junior elders to *Chuma* and the senior elders to *Maina* and *Nyongi*. Very few old men remained belonging to *Kimnyige*. According to traditional reckoning *Sawe* would have taken over military duties at a 'handing over' ceremony due in 1968.

22   This rendering is a literal translation from the Nandi.

23   The *nariet* headdress is the special headdress worn by a young woman coming out of seclusion; if the girl is a virgin it has tusks protruding from the front. A Christian version of the latter is the *sianya*.

24   The origin of the word '*king*' meaning 'stand' in this song probably lies in the standing for the British National Anthem when officialdom appeared to say 'king'.

25 The application of nettles to the breasts is purportedly to prevent irritation during the suckling of children.
26 Modern girls prefer money to gifts. This is understandable in view of the considerable expense to which the family may go to provide hospitality and gifts for the guests. The slaughter of a cow, sheep or goat is no longer sufficient or particularly cheap.
27 These two songs were collected by a friend in a former settlement area and the girl's name was Tapletgoi.
28 From the verb *tet*, meaning 'to set in order' or 'to set in order in a line'.
29 I was assured on this point by several doctors with extensive experience of Kalenjin women who had been circumcised. I observed for myself at Kapsowar hospital in Elgeyo-Marakwet District the severe effects of mutilation.
30 The ordeal is often minimised by the loud singing of the women to drown the girl's cries.
31 The Nandi 'betrothal' is not unlike the old ceremony of *sponsalia* which included the solemn troth-plight, the joining of hands and the giving and receiving of a ring or rings with certain gifts of money among its principal parts.
32 In the case of a man's first marriage a man's father with the help of suitable relatives, e.g. grandparents, maternal uncles, elders, etc. made the approaches. In the case of a second or subsequent marriage the man himself (unless his father was still alive) with the help of his senior wife and neighbourhood elders did so.
33 In Nandi respectively *senetwet* (a bushy plant or shrub of the cassia species) and *labotwet* (commonly known as the 'sodom apple').
34 This room is called *njor* and it is here that the negotiations take place.
35 During this period of her seclusion the initiand is clad in the *nyorgit* garb — a long leather skirt reaching from neck to ankles — and the *soiywet* headdress — a leather hood made so as to cover the head and shoulders with the exception of two little slots for the eyes to peer through. Quite commonly nowadays, this is replaced by *chepkauiyet*, covering the lower part of the body from the waist down, and a 'blouse' which can be extended over the head in the manner of a hood is worn around the shoulders.
36 *Labet-ab-eun*, literally, 'the stitching' or 'the sewing' of hands.
37 In Nandi *kamuiset*.
38 In Nandi *kapkiyai*, literally, 'the place of immersion'.
39 In Nandi *nilwet*, from the word *nge*, meaning 'thong'.
40 In Nandi *ng'ang'et*.
41 The headdress is called *nariet*, the bell *cheptingiliet* and the tusks *kelek* or *masarek*.

VI. Marriage

'The most formidable foe we have to face is their fearful immorality', wrote one of the early Nandi missionaries.[1] The first reactions of the ethnographer, J.A. Massam, to Keiyo practices were somewhat similar: 'They are polyandrous [sic], and they appear at first sight to have no moral code.'[2]

The initial reactions of these two men to Kalenjin sexual behaviour were typical of their age. But as Massam changed his first impressions:

That impression is not really correct. They have their standards, which are on the whole strictly observed —

so nowadays the contention of early evolutionists that man lived originally in a state of general promiscuity (and people such as the Kalenjin were of course 'carbon-copies' of early man) is considered nonsensical. Instead, it is generally recognised that from the beginning man developed some form of 'marriage' to aid his struggle for survival. And in an attempt to classify the many and varied relationships arising from such marriage he devised elaborate systems in which are to be observed many differences. Therefore, although to the first missionaries and travellers the Nandi may have appeared promiscuous they in fact possessed a well-ordered, even if somewhat unfamiliar, system of kinship and marriage.

1. Traditional Patterns of Kinship and Marriage

(i) The Family

The English word 'family' is derived from the Latin *familia*, meaning 'household'. In different societies and cultures relations group themselves into households according to different principles. The Nandi way of doing this is neither the grouping of the so-called 'nuclear' or 'conjugal' family where the husband-wife-children relationship is primary but rather the grouping of the 'extended' family or kindred group consisting of a series of close relatives along the male and female lines.

(a) The Polygamous Household. A Nandi proverb declares: 'No woman will be unmarried in her lifetime.'[3] The practice of polygamy assisted in the realisation of this ideal and probably in the distant past Nandi knew neither spinsters nor bachelors. Even nowadays the unmarried are known by a nickname probably meaning 'the barren ones'.[4]

A Nandi man could have as many wives as he could afford. And probably due to the political and economic structures of the tribe wealth tended to be distributed fairly evenly. Consequently, for a man to have two wives was common, three moderately so and more than three relatively rare. True, Hollis records that he knew the Kipsigis *Laibon* to have had twenty-eight wives and wealthy Nandi reputedly as many as forty.[5] These appear to be exceptional cases.

A man's first wife was his chief wife,[6] and he sought her approval before taking a second. Indeed, it was often one wife who chose another, a practice to be welcomed for the peaceful ordering of the household. The eldest son of the chief wife, although not necessarily the firstborn, was the senior son of the household.

Each wife had her own house from which she brought up her family and cultivated some of her husband's land. The husband visited his wives regularly.

(b) The Extended Family or Kindred Group.[7] The family of an individual Nandi comprised not only parents, siblings and children in direct line of descent but all members of his kindred group. To say *'Mii tiliet'* or *'Mamii tiliet'* — a man is or is not in the kindred group — expressed relationship in Nandi. The *tiliet*, as briefly mentioned earlier, was a kindred group akin to the Teutonic *sib*, somewhat ill-defined but including an individual's cognates and affines — those related to him by cognatic descent and marriage. All of these people a man called by relationship terms; those for whom he had no relationship terms were outside his kindred group.[8] The grouping is roughly paralleled among other Kalenjin people, for example the Kipsigis as described by Peristiany and the Marakwet as described by Kipkorir and Welbourn.[9]

Three general points should be noted: the system of kinship terminology was classificatory, of the type which anthropologists call bifurcate merging (when ego's father and one uncle, but not two, are described by the same term); terminology identified stratification according to generation; different forms were used for direct and indirect modes of address.

In the second and third ascending and descending generations grandfathers and their grandsons great-grandfathers and their great grandsons were *inguget* (direct form, *kugo*), great-grandmothers and their great-granddaughters *isenget* (direct form, *senge*); grandfathers and their grandsons were *inguget* (direct form, *agui*) and grandmothers and their granddaughters *ingoget* (direct form, *kogo*).

In the first ascending generation a father and his brothers were *kwan*, a mother and her sisters *kamet*, their wives and husbands being respectively *kamet* and *kwan*. A father's sisters were *isenget* (direct form, *senge*) and a mother's brothers *imamet* (direct form, *mama*), their husbands and wives being respectively *sandit* (or *sandana*) and *imamet*.

In the first descending generation children of a man and his brothers and sisters were *lakwet*.

In a man's own generation his brothers and sisters and parallel cousins were *tupchet* and their spouses *bamuru* with the exception of a sister's husband who was known as *sandit*. Cross-cousins on a father's father's side were *mama* and their spouses also *mama*. Cross-cousins on the mother's side did not have a uniform terminology: a mother's brother's son was *mama* and his wife *mama* while a mother's brother's daughter was *kamet* and her husband *kwan*.

In addition to the above, terms were employed dependent on whether the speaker was male or female and his references in the first, second or third person. Affines also came within the kindred group. A wife's father and his brothers were *kabyugoi*, a wife's mother and mother's sisters were *karujo*, a wife's father's sisters were *bamuru* and a wife's mother's brothers were *abuleiyo*. A husband's father was *bamong'o* and his mother *boger*.

Summarily, using ego-focus, a Nandi distinguished between four groups of people. Cognates were divided into *kapkwanit*, paternal kin, and *kabimamet*, maternal or mother's brother's kin. Affines were divided into *kapkatun*, the group into which a woman was married (wife's term) and *kabyugoi*, a man's father-in-law's group (husband's term).

Among an individual's relatives his maternal uncle played an important role. Boys in particular had to seek his consent before going through rituals such as *tumdo*. In return for kindness and concern a young warrior gave his maternal uncle a cow secured by raiding. But if a young Nandi displeased his maternal uncle the matter was viewed with the utmost gravity.[10]

(ii) *The Clan*[11]

The Nandi possess seventeen clans, five of which have more than one totem or sacred animal — *tiond ab oret*. Nowadays, the clans are dispersed throughout Nandi; it is supposed, however, that the clan took its origins in a patrilineal descent group from a common ancestor.

(iii) *Incest and Exogamy*

There are three exogamic groups in Nandi, the clan, the kindred group and the age-set. A man may not marry a woman belonging to his own clan unless it has more than one totem nor may he marry a woman from certain other clans with which marriage is forbidden. A man may not marry a woman from his own kindred group, that is, a woman whom he calls by a relationship term. A man may not marry the daughter of a man belonging to his own age-set, the set into which his own children are being circumcised — it would be like marrying his own daughter. (If marriage were to occur unwittingly between members of these exogamic groups then the elders examined the case and if the relationship was considered too close dissolved the marriage.)

Likewise, sexual intercourse between members of the same group was considered incestuous. There was clan incest, kindred group incest and age-set incest. Incest was viewed very seriously indeed if the couple were closely related, for example a girl and her maternal or paternal uncle.[12]

(iv) *Sexual Relations*

(*a*) *Premarital Sex*. As we have already seen, after circumcision the young warriors were free to engage in intercrural sex play with young uncircumcised girls in their communal hut. It was a great shame for both the girl and her 'sweetheart' if she became pregnant. The child of such an illicit union was either smothered or strangled before it could take its first breath.[13] The mother became unclean and remained so for the rest of her life.[14] She might however be married by members of some clans; for example, except for his first wife, a man of the 'Soldier Ant' clan preferred a girl who had already conceived, and did not object to his own daughters conceiving before marriage.[15]

(*b*) *Extramarital Sex*. Without being considered guilty of a sexual offence, a married woman might continue after her marriage to have sexual intercourse with her old 'sweetheart' from the communal hut. Moreover, when a man gave hospitality to a member of the subdivision of his own age-set he abandoned his house and allowed his wife and his age-mate to have intercourse. These two categories aside, a married woman was forbidden extramarital sex. If a man caught his wife infringing the rules he could try to divorce her if childless, or beat her and the male offender if possible. The offence was termed *chor konget*, 'the woman is stolen'. Of course, habitual beating of his wife might lead to a husband's being reported to her father or brothers and ultimately deserted.

(*c*) *Rape*. This was considered an outrage on the female sex. According to Snell, a warrior guilty of this offence was beaten by members of his own age-set and denied certain social privileges such as jumping in the middle of the ring during circumcision festivities. An older man was treated with social contempt or if guilty of causing an abortion had severe punishment meted out to him.[16]

(*d*) *Homosexuality*. According to Snell such offences were very rare. Personally I found very little knowledge of such affairs. An offender caught in the act could be killed. Otherwise, he was beaten by members of his age-set or if his case was considered serious cursed by neighbourhood elders and held up to social ridicule.[17]

(v) *Child Marriage*

I have not personally encountered this among the Nandi but record the practice as described by Huntingford:

Sometimes a girl is married when very young, before puberty and before she is circumcised. Such marriages take place for economic reasons, as when a poor man with a very young daughter needs cattle for helping his son to marry. He may arrange the marriage with a married friend who is willing to pay the cattle. After marriage, the girl is dressed as a married woman, and lives under the care of her husband's first wife till she is sent to circumcision, when she is given a hut of her own. Should she conceive before going, she is circumcised at once, and thus avoids the lot of the *cesorpucot* or girl who conceives before circumcision.[18]

An informant told me that the practice is not known at present, but that the child of a poor family was married when beginning to grow permanent teeth and maybe a cow was received as part of the bride-wealth used for feeding until the child was matured and ready to be handed over to her husband. Nowadays, he said, such an act would be considered 'bribery' rather than a down-payment.[19]

(vi) *The Levirate*

Among the Nandi marriage was indissoluble even in death so that a widow could never remarry.

Yet the Nandi practised the levirate, calling it *kindi*, meaning 'the inheriting'. On the death of a woman's husband it fell to his junior brother nearest him in age (or in the event of his immaturity the next eldest) to be responsible for the care of his widow.[20] This involved, as well as the physical protection of his person, children and property, the maintenance and rebuilding of her house, cultivation and fencing of her land, care of her cattle and representation in any neighbourhood discussion. But it was only with her consent that the brother-in-law acquired rights *in uxorem*. Here Nandi custom bears out the contemporary insistence that widows never were inherited and neither was the levirate ever looked upon as remarriage. Rather the custom was intended to care for widows — their personal, family or domestic, sexual and procreative needs — within the context of the kindred group into which they married.[21]

In accordance with this principle there was no compulsion for a widow to seek her brother-in-law's protection. Particularly if she were rich and had sons to inherit she needed no proxy- or surrogate husband but lived an independent existence eventually being cared for by her youngest son who built his house near hers, although the general management of family affairs fell to the eldest. Moreover, if the deceased left more than one wife, only the junior wife was expected to cohabit with her late husband's brother.

Since the circumcision of the present *Sawe* generation the levirate is looked upon with distaste and is resorted to only in secret; 'No woman wants to be the slave of another woman', I was told.

Children of a childless widow resorting to the levirate inherited from the dead man — *pater* — and not from the biological father — *genitor*. It was the eldest son who inherited and if feeling generous shared with the next in seniority. But if the widow had heirs by her first marriage the children of the subsequent union, *kindi*, inherited from their biological father.

(vii) *Woman Marriage — 'relighting the fire of the clan'*[22]

When a childless couple became too old for child-bearing, a childless woman widowed, or a childless wife unable to conceive, two serious questions arose. Who would inherit the land and property? Who would perpetuate the lineage? In addition to the obvious answer of polygamy, in some instances the interesting expedient of woman marriage was resorted to. The childless woman took to wife a younger woman and raised children either to her own or her husband's clan. The children's genitor was an approved visitor, that is, approved by the childless woman, her own family and her husband's family. It was not required that the genitor be unmarried. Probably the usual rules of exogamy applied as the two women went through the full marriage ceremony.[23] The practice is to be distinguished from 'ghost marriage' where the young woman is reckoned to be the wife of the deceased. In Nandi the 'marriage' is between the two women. Nowadays, when the older or childless woman is a spinster she often allows the younger woman to choose her lover. The practice is common; I know of no area of Nandi which I visited without hearing of an example in the neighbourhood. At Arwos in central Nandi there was in 1973 a woman of substance with three younger 'wives'. The most interesting case to me was a spinster (Nandi) living in Keiyo country, a member of the Africa Inland Church, who appeared to the local population to have her 'niece' and her children living with her. She was in fact married to the younger woman, a Kipsigis, the children's genitor being a prominent businessman and farmer. The children called the older woman *kogo*, signifying 'grandmother', a custom which I find intriguing but for which I have been unable to trace any expressed reason.

(viii) *'Marriage into the House'*[24]

Also underlining the importance of inheritance is a recent innovation — the custom came in with the children of the present *Maina* age-set about twenty years ago. In order to ensure that the inheritance is kept within a family into which only daughters have been born, either the only, youngest or favourite daughter remains at home unmarried and is visited by a genitor from outside. When sons have been raised to the household she is free to get married and leave. As no man may be taken onto the ancestral land, the practice keeps property within the family and clan. The change may have been brought about by Christians anxious to avoid polygamy; but it is also resorted to by widows with daughters only: they keep the youngest daughter to be 'married into the house'.[25]

(ix) *Bridewealth — 'the cattle of the girl'*[26]

My first encounter with the institution of bridewealth among the Nandi was during student seminars in 1967 when I listened to young men as they lamented the steep rise in the amount of stock and cash being demanded, and expressed their despair of ever being able to 'afford a wife'. For them, the abuse of a worthy traditional institution had brought very real problems.

Abuse it most certainly was, for traditionally even a man so poor as not to be able to afford any bridewealth might leave his bow and arrow at the door of his prospective father-in-law's house — a guarantee that he was an able-bodied warrior capable of raiding cattle which he would hand over later. It was not considered lucky for a man to refuse such a guarantee. Often, the debt incurred by marriage was not paid until much later as for example in the following instance related to me by a schoolgirl.[27] At the end of the last century her grandfather left his bow and arrows and shield at the door of her grandmother's father's house. The marriage took place, but in 1965 or 1966, so Elisaba relates, her father paid three cattle (his mother's bridewealth) to his mother's relatives. Thus, more than sixty years elapsed between a woman's marriage and the paying of her bridewealth by her son.

Bridewealth, in Nandi, is not *per se* necessary to the completion of marriage. It is more than anything else the ratification of an alliance between two kinship groups. Two things point to this interpretation: the symbolism of the marriage ritual and the origin of the animals originally given as bridewealth. The former we shall describe in detail and interpret later, the latter can be summarised briefly here. In a typical handing over of bridewealth comprising three cattle and three sheep or goats one of the cattle came from the suitor, another from his father's sister and the third from one of his married sisters already a mother; one of the sheep or goats also came from the suitor, another from his father's sister and the third from either his father or grand-father.[28]

In 1902, according to H.H. Johnston, the 'price' paid to the father of the bride among the Nandi was 'four goats, a fowl, and a cow'; in 1905-8, according to A.C. Hollis, it was one bull, one cow and ten goats; between 1924 and 1941, according to G.W.B. Huntingford, the average number of stock given in bridewealth was one ox or bull, one cow, three goats or three sheep. I made a note from the Africa Inland Church records at Kapsabet of detailed information concerning amounts agreed to by Christian families between the years 1926 and 1967. Over these forty years the bridewealth had just about doubled, for example, from one heifer, one barren cow and one bull in 1927 to two oxen and four cows in 1964, but, interestingly enough, one important new factor had been introduced — the cash payment — at first ostensibly for the purpose of buying stock.[29] Figures which I collected in 1973 indicated that at least in practice the bridewealth had become very much greater, for example, two cows plus 500 shillings, four to six cows plus 1,000 shillings, or even sixteen cows plus 4,000 shillings.

Payments by instalment were the exception, although there is a term, *chebager*, which designates the token animal given as earnest in such a method of payment. Moreover, if the woman failed to bear children then the bridewealth was returnable. On the other hand, if she died having borne children, but before the completion of bridewealth payment, her husband and family had to complete the payment.

2. *The Marriage Ritual*[30]

(i) *The Giving of the Bride*[31]

Three, perhaps seven, days before the date fixed for the wedding, marriage preparations begin in the homes of both bride and bridegroom. The master of ceremonies, or to be more specific, the wedding elder, and two sponsors, one male and one female, are chosen.[32] The female sponsor in particular is likely to be one of those who instructed the bride during *tumdo* and the man may be either her husband or one of those who instructed the bridegroom or even another suitable person. Both must belong to the age-set of the bridegroom's father. Two other ritual personages are required, however, for weddings; a young boy and a young girl aged between four and eleven years approximately — the years when boys learn to herd cattle and girls learn to look after their younger brothers and sisters. The girl is known as 'nursemaid' and will carry a gourd full of milk on her back symbolising a baby; the boy is known as 'shepherd' or 'herdsboy' and will carry a stick appropriate to his task and symbolising the male role of cattle-keeping.[33]

The bridegroom's family then set aside a ceremonial house,[34] prepare beer and slaughter an ox for the wedding feast. The bride's family, meanwhile, arrange for the girl to burn some ritual plants at the shrine and prepare the household effects and wedding garments. One day before the actual ritual begins they may travel and stay overnight at the bridegroom's home. But this is not necessary.

While the bride's family, particularly the womenfolk, may go to stay at the bridegroom's home, similarly, one day before the wedding the bridegroom's sister (if possible the girl with whom he has the special *bamwai* relationship since *tumdo*) goes to the home of the bride to fetch her. According to some accounts she may be accompanied by or replaced by the bridegroom's mother — her future mother-in-law — and by two sponsors. Some informants say that on occasions the 'herdsboy' and 'nursemaid' accompany this party. Very early in the morning the bridal procession sets out for the bridegroom's home, that is if the journey is to be a long one and undertaken on foot. If a short journey only is required, deliberate delay may be made on the way. Often, nowadays, it is made by car or by bus. But the party must not arrive at its destination until late afternoon, preferably at 6 p.m. when the cows are being brought home from grazing. The party proceeds in ritual order led by the sponsors and bridegroom's sister (or mother as the case may be); friends and neighbours of the bride follow after, the younger ones bringing up the rear. Those young and unmarried must turn back before reaching the house of *tumdo* — Nandi weddings are for the initiated only. The bride or her assistant will carry a gourd of milk and a variety of household effects such as pots and pans and, nowadays, even the cat! She or some other member of the party will also carry the ritual ox-horn of clarified butter covered with a cloth.[35]

The bride, *kipkeleldet*, wears a dressed skin, decorated with coloured beads and reaching from waist to ankles, together with a warrior's cloak of calfskin, goatskin or sheepskin, thrown over one shoulder.[36] On her head she wears the *nariet* headdress made of leather and wire, decorated with cowrie shells and with a long leather strap and small bell attached and passing down the back through the belt.[37] If a virgin she also wears the ritual tusks above her forehead as on her coming out from *tumdo*. Her body is anointed and her hair dressed with red ochre.

On arrival at the bridegroom's home the bridal party is welcomed by his family and the master of ceremonies. Then, until the appointed time for the ceremony — this varies according to clan regulations — the bride and groom are individually closeted in separate houses and given instruction by the sponsors and elders. The instruction concerns ritual procedure. Meanwhile, guests are drinking beer and feasting.[38]

(ii) *The Marriage*[39]

Among the Keiyo, *katunisiet* is the third in a series of marriage rituals; it takes place in the eighth or ninth month of the woman's first pregnancy and is marked by feasting and the giving to the bride of a ring.[40] Among the Marakwet, *katunisio* is a second and major stage which can take place only after the birth of a child; it is an expensive feast and is often postponed so long that a son may have to arrange it for his own mother as none of a man's children can marry until *katunisio* has been performed for their mother.[41] Similarly, among the Kipsigis, *katunisiet* is a beer and food festival which takes place many months and possibly years after the giving of the cattle which in turn takes place three or many more years after the initial 'binding' of a Kipsigis couple.[42] Likewise, too, among the Terik, marriage rituals are not completed until after a child has been born of the union. Among the Nandi, however, *katunisiet* is the term applied to the total sequence of marriage rituals, apart from the preliminary betrothal during the engagement visit. *Katunisiet* lasts for two or three days and embraces several rites separated by months and years among other Kalenjin peoples.[43]

When the appointed time for the actual marriage ritual arrives, the bridegroom wearing a warrior's animal skin cloak (which passes under his right armpit and over the left shoulder where it is tied by means of short straps) is brought by his sponsor and master of ceremonies to meet his bride. Then, led by the sponsor and followed by the 'herds-boy' and 'nursemaid', bride and bridegroom process in ritual order four times around the shrine. The first time round they are spat on with milk from a small children's gourd by a warrior appointed for the task.[44] Then, inside the ceremonial house they are issued with some further instructions as to ritual procedure while the guests continue drinking beer and eating meat and porridge. Younger guests drink milk as, traditionally, beer-drinking is the prerogative of age and seniority.

It appears from some accounts that where the custom of employing a 'herdsboy' and 'nursemaid' has fallen into disuse the bride or an appointed assistant carries the milk gourd on her back. In describing the ritual I shall assume the presence of the young 'herdsboy' and 'nursemaid' attendants — too young to remember important ritual details or understand their significance.

Inside the ceremonial house the company is assembled singing around a ritual beer-pot in the centre of the room. The bride's family sits on the left or female side of the house (as one enters), the bride-groom's on the right or male side, if possible father sitting opposite father, mother opposite mother and so on. Only as many relatives as can fit in the animal compartment — the eastern room — with the wedding elders and bridal party are present. The bridal pair, flanked on either side by the 'herdsboy' and 'nursemaid' and their two sponsors, are placed beside the beer-pot in the centre and faced by the master of ceremonies dressed in his colobus monkey skin cloak.[45]

The gourd on the 'nursemaid's' back and the stick in the 'herds-boy's' hand symbolise respectively their function as children's nurse and herder of flocks. At this stage, the bride and groom are expected to act as father and mother to the two children. While the 'mother' cooks food for her husband the 'nursemaid' looks after the children and the 'father' instructs his 'herdsboy' son in the care of the flocks. Thus, a fruitful marriage is ritually anticipated by enacted or dramatised symbolism.[46]

The couple then kneels, holding in front of them in both pairs of hands a knotty *nogirwet* stick — symbol of fertility — brought to the ceremony by the master of ceremonies. (The stick, twined round with ritual creeper, is given to the bridegroom and a gourd and cleaning stick given to the bride afterwards.)[47] Beer is spilled on the stick by the master of ceremonies and milk by the bride's father. And then, as the couple circumambulate the beer-pot four times — still on their knees and holding the stick — the company sings songs wishing the couple a fruitful and happy marriage. If the ritual grass has not been stepped on at betrothal it is stepped on now by both partners, and a sheep promised to the bride.[48] Some accounts assert that the father of the bride gives her hand in marriage to the bridegroom, others that the master of ceremonies hooks the little fingers of bride and bridegroom. I am not convinced that if this is so it is not due to Christian and western influence. Be that as it may, the most important part of the ceremony is yet to be performed. The bride and bridegroom are seated on a black and white goatskin. The sponsors, in possession of the strands of ritual grass, exchange strands, plait them and tie them four times on the left wrist of the bride and on the right wrist of the bridegroom. Alternatively, if some accounts are to be believed, the bride's ring is put round her neck, but it is unlikely that plaited strands of the ritual grass would be long enough to form a necklace. The master of ceremonies then takes his little ritual gourd, dips it in a small pot of unrefined beer and sucks through the small hole in its side a mouthful of beer which he spits out in a fine spray on the couple, adding at the end the blessing *'Sere'* (literally, 'Be blessed').[49] Meanwhile, the company sings marriage songs. One such song special to some groups and not always sung is called *Ayamoing* and alludes to a boat crossing over to the other side: the bride has gone to her husband, a member of one clan has joined another.[50]

Whether or not the two young attendants are always present for the 'tying of the grass' is not clear. Some say 'Yes' others 'No'. Those asserting that they are present throughout explain this as the reason for their being as young as possible: they will retain neither knowledge nor understanding of the ritual; and this is as it should be because the rituals are intended for the married only.[51] However, for the next part of the procedure they are definitely in attendance. They produce the ritual ox-horn of clarified butter and the stick for its application. It is applied first to bride and groom and the sponsors; this is followed by the mutual anointing of opposite numbers in the kindred group —

father anoints father, mother mother and so on. All say '*Bamwai*' and the new relationship between all members of the kindred group is established. No longer will names be used but relationship terms. Now, the ritual beer-drink to cement the new relationships may be engaged in. First, the master of ceremonies, then the sponsors, then the bride and bridegroom and finally all in the house drink from the communal beer-pot, using the long drinking tubes.[52] Fellowship is complete.

The beer-drink over, the 'herdsboy' and 'nursemaid' are dismissed, fed, and sent to bed. So too, the parents of the couple are asked to leave, elders only remaining. According to one colourful account the hide of an ox recently skinned is placed standing to form an arch in the room and the bride and bridegroom enter through the arch four times. There follows the act of ritual intercourse, which evokes comments from the onlookers.[53] Instruction follows.

At this point I ought to make clear the lack of uniformity in practice from the 'tying of the grass' onwards. If the girl is a virgin, ritual intercourse and much instruction may be very necessary so that for the whole of the following day the bride remains by the animal compartment burning ritual plants while the bridegroom walks about with his age-mates and the guests engage in feasting and drinking. The instruction is resumed the following night. However, where nowadays the girl is not a virgin or may even be pregnant, ritual intercourse and related instruction are not deemed necessary. These variations, also the fact that under the influence of Christianity ritual intercourse is not considered seemly, explain why the duration of the marriage rituals varies from twenty-four to forty-eight hours. (For the duration of the marriage ritual and for some time afterwards, until the newly-weds' house has been built and set in readiness, the bridegroom's father and mother give up their own house and sleep in the grain store or other suitable building nearby.)

After the tying of the grass a bonfire is lit outside the ceremonial house by the shrine and the bridal pair engage in the fourfold ritual procession. When they return inside, drinking and feasting may continue until dawn.

If on the first night ritual intercourse takes place after the tying of the grass, then on the following night the couple go to sleep at opposite sides of the animal compartment. They sleep, with the *chepkosinet* gourd and the *sosiot* stick, the *kelek* headdress and *kaplonginet* arrow by their sides, on *muita* — an ox skin — and are covered by *kiboet*.

Very early the following morning bride and mother-in-law go to the river to bathe, the bride bringing back some water for her husband in a small pot.[54] Breakfast is served by the bridegroom's mother, usually comprising milk, possibly from the ritual gourd used during the ritual of the previous night.

In the past, but not usually nowadays, a goat was slaughtered and its entrails examined to judge the omens.[55]

The parts of the ceremony thus described are followed according to Hollis by events lasting up to four days. These events are now telescoped into a few hours. However, it is necessary to quote Hollis for completeness:

> Soon after sunset the bridegroom conducts the bride to a friend's house, which has been prepared for them. After she has entered, he performs the duties otherwise performed by the wife, closing the door, making the beds, and attending to the fire. The marriage may not yet be consummated.
>
> The next morning the bride opens the door and cooks some food for her husband, whilst her mother brings milk and assists her. The girl also brings water with which to wash his hands, and a stool for him to sit on; but he refuses to have anything to do with her. At length, after she has promised him the cow her father has given her, he consents to allow her to wait on him, but he will not touch the food until one of his friends (of the same *mat* as himself) has been brought in to taste it. He then eats and drinks, and that night the marriage is consummated.
>
> Four days later the bridal pair move into their own house, and for a whole month are waited on by the bridegroom's mother, as it is unlawful for the bride during this period to work.[56]

Hollis has omitted some ritual details and I shall continue my account from the breakfast onwards.

At the shrine the hair of both bride and groom is shaven and their grass bracelets untied.[57] Hair and grass are mixed together and then the hair separated from the grass again. The hair is mixed with cowdung and smeared round the base of the shrine while the ritual grass is first dropped in the animal compartment then retrieved and placed in a ritual ox-horn to be taken by the bridegroom's mother and kept until two children have been born of the union (covered in cowdung in a small pot and stored in the loft).[58] After that it may be discarded. But if no children are born then the ritual grass may be brought from the loft and divorce and return of the bridewealth demanded.

The bride's family will have been shown the bridewealth before the beginning of the ceremonies but now comes the ritual examination. Members of both families carry sticks of the species *diospyres abyssinica* or *cassia didymobotrya* with which to hit the animal.[59] First, the bridegroom hits the cow straight on the back and the brother of the bride and other relatives do likewise in turn. It may be when the father of the bridegroom hits up to three animals on the stomach, denoting that he wants their young, that the bride's father refuses: he may have one of the young but in ordinary circumstances no more.

During the afternoon, the bride, especially if she is a virgin, receives presents of animals and household effects. One Christian mother told me how her daughter, a virgin, received eight cattle in honour of her virginity.

Whether on that evening or the following the bridegroom and his bride go to their own house, the bride now cooks for her husband. It is a special stiff porridge stirred with a wooden spoon and made of finger millet meal.[60] Meanwhile, the husband stays about forty yards away with his bow and sword by the side of the door. As the food is ready he places his implements inside. The wife approaches with a pot of water with which to wash his hands but he ritually refuses until one of his age-mates agrees to wash and eat first, and the bride agrees to give him the cow promised to her by her father-in-law.[61] The food is piled high in a small basket, made of palm leaves, and later placed on a round piece of skin.[62] The food, likened by many of the younger Nandi to the western wedding-cake, is called *kipsongiot* and is cut with a wooden knife and eaten with the fingers while fermented milk is drunk from a gourd.[63] Yet, despite this ritual meal, for the next three weeks it is the bride's mother-in-law who cooks for her son and daughter-in-law.

That afternoon or next day when the feasting is over, the presents given and the livestock examined, the bride's family party sets out in procession and in single file on the journey home. The journey is called *kayomiset* and those undertaking it carry with them gifts of six to eight large gourds of milk and a basket of millet from the bridegroom's family.

One final matter needs to be settled. After about two weeks — or when the hair of bride and groom has grown — the family of the bride sends a child to enquire after the bridewealth.[64] The son-in-law is then sent to collect either the first instalment or the total bridewealth (according to what has been agreed).[65] The son-in-law helps to drive the cattle and animals to the road and men drive them away. The next message is 'The girl wants to visit home.'[66] This is the signal requesting the sending of *chepsinendet* and *chepng'abait*. The former is the sheep tied with *sinendet* going to the person who fed the bride during her seclusion (mother or otherwise) and the latter the sheep due to the person who ground the meal (mother or maybe neighbour of the parents if they had no meal). If *chepng'abait* is given to a neighbour from whom flour was borrowed then the lambs will go to the bride's father.

The new couple may settle either patrilocally or neolocally at some distance; traditionally, however, a younger son settled near his mother as his was the responsibility for caring for her in her old age.

3. *Changing Patterns of Kinship and Marriage*

(i) *Sexual Promiscuity*

Luo and Swahili folk songs extolling the beauties of Nandi women — these, if nothing else, serve to make us acutely aware of how idealised present-day accounts of traditional Nandi marriage customs have become.[67] Nevertheless, the structures are there, and we may therefore assume a certain measure of stability until the 'coming of the Europeans'.[68]

There is, to my mind, adequate evidence to suggest change in the direction of sexual promiscuity with the coming of 'Arabs', Indians and Europeans to Nandi.

First, in the 1850s, when the *Sawe* generation of warriors was in office, attempts were made by 'Arabs' to 'interfere with women and girls'; so writes A.T. Matson.[69]

Secondly, the coolies employed in the construction of the Uganda Railway abducted Nandi boys and girls:

Apart from the squalor, they [the coolie camps] were crowded with prostitutes, small boys, and other accessories to the bestial vices so commonly practised by Orientals. Complaints by the Nandi and Lumbwa natives were frequent, Lumbwa becoming so restive on account of so many of their young women being inveigled away from their homes, and harboured in those sinks of iniquity ...

so writes F.J. Jackson.[70]

Thirdly, Sudanese soldiers and European administrators, particularly during the period of Nandi resistance to British rule (1890-1906), kept Nandi concubines, as is evidenced by even such a partisan observer as Colonel R. Meinertzhagen:

[Commenting on the arrival of the administrator Mayes' 'wife' from Mauritius on 13 April 1905 he writes:]

It is all a bit difficult, as Mayes has half a dozen Nandi concubines in the house. I left them to fight it out among themselves ...

[And later] I have had so many complaints from natives about the way in which Mayes is robbing them of their cattle, sheep, goats and even girls that I have embodied them all in a report to Baggs, the Sub-Commissioner at Kisumu.[71]

Fourthly, and this is hardly surprising in view of the foregoing, there is ample proof in government records of growing administrative anxiety about the spread of venereal disease in Kenya.

At national level the *Handbook of Kenya Colony and Protectorate* states on page 340:

This [venereal disease and syphilis] is also, unhappily spreading. In 1915 the hospital cases were as follows: from the mountain zone, 410 (syphilis) and 316 (gonorrhoea); from Kenya and Nyanza provinces, 312 (syphilis) and 197 (gonorrhoea).[72]

At provincial level John Ainsworth, Provincial Commissioner of Nyanza (which included Nandi District), writes in his Annual Report for 1911-12:

Syphilis is unfortunately very much on the increase amongst the natives in Nandi and Lumbwa, and to an extent in Kisii. It is also evident amongst the Kavirondo. Amongst the Lumbwa and Nandi its spread is due to the immorality of the women who leave the Reserve to lead a loose life at various centres up and down the Railway line. The Chiefs and Elders have been strongly advised to prevent the women from leaving the villages and latterly, I believe, our advice is having some effect. It is, however, rather late, as the disease has already obtained a firm hold in the Nandi and Lumbwa areas ... Kisii — possibly from Government stations and Trading Centres ... Kavirondo — women extremely moral with strangers but not with own people. Maybe because able bodied men go to work not taking women ... It would seem desirable to treat syphilis as a contagious disease requiring even more drastic treatment as regards segregation than plague. The matter is without doubt a serious one and requires very serious consideration.[73]

At district level, one official after another writes along the following lines, often with statistics to support opinions:

There are no prevailing diseases calling for any special remarks with the exception of venereal which appears to be spreading rapidly as is bound to prove the case amongst a tribe having social customs such as prevail amongst the Nandi. (QR, 31/12/'09.)[74]

I pursued the subject further in 1969, and found that the Medical Officer of Health in Nandi was concerned about an outbreak of venereal diseases in 1968 and the inadequacy of treatment being offered privately by former medical dressers.[75] He viewed the situation with the utmost gravity but explained how it was much easier for the authorities to give priority to a current epidemic of tuberculosis; venereal disease was considered more in the nature of a social problem and therefore more difficult to eradicate.

Similarly, the comments made by schoolboys in a questionnaire which I administered in 1973 left me in no doubt as to the general promiscuity of their behaviour. This conclusion was supported by an estimated 5 per cent pregnancy rate among Nandi girls in secondary schools in the District (this excludes abortions) and a very much higher rate (reportedly at times 75 per cent) among primary schoolgirls. There is no indication that the situation is any better among those not attending school: I have known many unmarried mothers from all three categories. One explanation is to be found in the disappearance of the warriors' communal hut and its discipline of intercrural intercourse.

(ii) *Prostitution*

One of the reasons advanced to me against the theory that the purpose of clitoridectomy was to curb sexual excitement and desire was the incidence of prostitution among Nandi women. In other words, to Nandi men, clitoridectomy did not appear to lessen the desire of their women for other men. A.T. Matson makes the point that during the nineteenth century Nandi wars with neighbouring peoples, particularly the Maasai and Luyia, were punctuated by truces in times of famine. During such truces the womenfolk travelled into neighbouring areas to barter for food.[76] It has been suggested that in these journeyings of Nandi women can be found the first signs of prostitution. Thus by 1909 (as C.H. Stigand remarks), Nandi women had become 'notorious from Mombasa to Kisumu'. The year 1909 was also the year by which the Nandi Hut and Poll Tax had to be paid in cash and prostitution was a ready means of obtaining such.[77] It comes then as nothing of a surprise to read in the Annual Report for 1913: 'The most enlightened members of the tribe appear to be the prostitutes who have spent some time in Nairobi or elsewhere.' Thereafter, prostitution continued to grow apace, providing, according to Alice Gold, 'a necessary and accepted prop to the sometimes strained Nandi economy'[78] so that by 1935 it was, if anything, more widespread. This is indicated by a report written by the then District Commissioner of Nandi, Captain F.D. Hislop, and entitled 'Report of our Enquiries Regarding Nandi Morality' and subsumed under the heading 'X: Anthropological' of the Annual Report for 1935.[79]

Today the problem continues, being much aggravated by the rapid growth of small trading centres throughout the District in the past fifteen years and the mobility of the people due to settlement in the old European farming areas.

Some of the reasons for the rise and growth of prostitution are obvious from the foregoing but its peculiar propensity among the Nandi women cannot be fully understood without reference to the patriarchal nature of Nandi society and its relationship to divorce regulations, to be discussed in the next chapter.

(iii) *Polygamy*

There is no way of accurately measuring the extent of polygamy at the beginning of this century. It is most probable that Hollis exaggerated the number of wives possessed by any one man. Basing his findings on researches carried out between 1926 and 1948, G.W.B. Huntingford in 1953 estimated that a man seldom had more than two or at most three wives. As for the extent of the practice, he estimated a probable 10 per cent. In November 1973, however, I personally conducted a survey of 883 families with children at primary school and found that thirty-one per cent of these families were polygamous. Consequently, I have reason to doubt Huntingford's figures, unless an initial decrease in the incidence of polygamy (with the coming of Christianity and a western life-style) has been halted and an increase initiated with the acquisition of new wealth. Certainly, I have first hand evidence of a revival of polygamy among Christians. According to various church

Memo.

KENYA

Dept.

9 - JAN 1936

19___

I, Kipkoech arap Murgei, hereby renounce any claim to Jebet d/o Kimais, to whom I was formerly married by native law and custom, and agree that this marriage is dissolved.

Kipkocch @ muio

Before me

[signature]

hap ″

18. Marriage dissolution.

19. Christian wedding, the bride wearing a Christian version of the virgin's headdress. (By kind permission of the Saina family.)

leaders, 15-20 per cent of church marriages turn polygamous. Moreover, I know of one of the leading churches belonging to the Africa
Inland Church where all the elders have taken second wives. I know of
a group of twelve established Christian men who moved out of the
District to form a co-operative in a former settlement area; only two
now maintain any link with the church and at least two have taken a
second wife. I know also that in May 1974 a Christian woman committed suicide rather than allow her husband, an elder in the church,
to take a young secondary schoolgirl to wife. Often a man has a wife on
the old ancestral plot in Nandi, a second in business at a local trading
centre or in town, and a third on a new farm in Uasin Gishu or Trans-
Nzoia. If therefore we take this question of newly-acquired wealth
together with an increase in bridewealth (making it difficult for young
men to marry) then it is possible at least quantitatively if not propor-
tionately that there has been an increase in polygamy in Nandi since
the early 1960s.

Among the Nandi today the largest families are to be found in the
Muslim community. The usual number of wives is 3-4, but I know of
at least one man in Kaptumo who in his lifetime had seven (some of
them successively, in accordance with Islamic law).[80]

(iv) *Monogamy*

Christian missionaries and colonial administrators introduced the
monogamous union and so-called 'nuclear family' into Nandi.
Because from the first some missionaries did not regard customary
marriage as 'marriage in the eyes of God',[81] they encouraged the
breaking of strained traditional unions in order that one or other of
the parties might be married to a Christian in church. Consequently,
for the Nandi, the issues became confused at two points: the new-
comers appeared to misunderstand the Nandi concept of 'family' and
the polygamous household and not believe in the indissolubility of
marriage. It is not surprising, therefore, that many Nandi Christians
even now do not fully comprehend the steps taken when entering into
a monogamous union. Take the following example. While investigat-
ing some statistics at the office of the Registrar General of Marriages in
Nairobi I was able to clarify for the Registrar why a Nandi woman had
approached him for a certificate of marriage. She was the wife of a
prominent government official, married in church. But her husband
had subsequently been married civilly (bigamously of course) a second
time and by customary law a third time.

If, with Adrian Hastings, we take the average number of marriages
per annum per thousand of the population to be eight and look at the
Nandi figures for Christian marriages the results are significant.[82] In
1969, the AIC rate was 3.0, the Catholic 4.4; in 1970, the AIC rate
was 1.9 and the Catholic 3.7.[83] In other words, normally not many

more than 50 per cent and sometimes less than 25 per cent of Christians in Nandi marry in church; by far the greatest number marry according to customary law. Moreover, as we have seen, 15-20 per cent of those married in church take second wives at a subsequent date.

Perhaps one of the most obvious reasons for this breakdown in marriage structures has been the insistence of missionaries that a polygamist wishing to be baptised must send away all but one wife. There is no evidence in Nandi that this caused great hardship or led to prostitution, because in the case of the AIC not many already married by customary law came to be married in church and in the case of the Catholic Church (according to Fr Kuhn) provision was made for former wives in the form of housing and a living allowance. In fact, some figures are worth quoting at this point. In the twenty years between 1932 and 1951, of the 117 marriages of Nandi in the AIC only five (4.27%) were remarriages in church of couples who had been married previously by Nandi customary law. During the same period in the same church, of a total of 213 Kalenjin of other tribes seventy-three (29.16%) were remarried in church. (This prompts the question as to whether or not this had anything to do with a distinctive factor in Nandi marriage, i.e. indissolubility.) On the other hand, in the next twenty years, 1952-71 (particularly after the impact of the East African Revival was felt in Nandi), 268 out of a total of 651 (41.16%) Nandi marriages were remarriages in church after an initial marriage by customary law.

Today, the older mission churches are facing the dilemma while a late arrival such as the Finnish Pentecostal Mission marries polygamists who show persistent signs of Christian faith.

(v) *Fertility*

One of the unresolved enigmas of population density in western Kenya is the smallness of Nandi families compared with those of the neighbouring Luo and Luyia. About 1890, it is estimated that the average number of children in a Luo family was 10.6, in a Luyia family 7.75 and in a Nandi family 2.6.[84] I suggest a variety of reasons: the late marriage of Nandi women, 25-30 years (and possibly later), and men, 30-40 years; the killing of illegitimate children; mutilation of the genitals during clitoridectomy (debatable as to incidence); the woman's role of journeying for food in times of famine; Nandi pride which did not wish more people than could be provided for without subservience to others.[85]

In 1973 I estimated the average family size as between 8-10. Obviously, physiologically, there is no reason why Nandi women should produce less children than others. Consequently, there has been growth in the live birth rate with the onset of modern conditions; for example, the use of vaccination, western medical treatment and habits of hygiene generally, and in particular the abandonment of the two-year gap between the birth of one child and the conception of another.

(vi) *Exogamy*

The rules are becoming less strictly observed as young people from prohibited clans do not see any reason why they ought not to marry.

(vii) *The Family*

In this area the changes are far-reaching. Men work in towns, visiting their families only at week-ends or at intervals of many months. The boys, consequently, will see their father, who in traditional life was their instructor, only very occasionally. As already mentioned, a man's wives can live many miles apart, with the women who live at trading centres often engaging in prostitution and concubinage. The development in practice of the 'conjugal' or 'mother-child' family, consequently is to be widely observed. With such changes the character of the 'extended' family changes too.

(viii) *Bridewealth*

The most significant change in this area, apart from the increase in amount and the substitution of cash for cattle already mentioned, is the turning of what was formerly the cementing of a kinship alliance into a monetary transaction, the purpose of which is often seen nowadays to be compensation or payment for the education of a daughter. Thus the young men are faced with sometimes insuperable obstacles to marriage in their youth. It is easy to understand why parents will prefer to give their daughter to be the second or third wife of a wealthy old farmer or businessman rather than the first wife of a struggling junior clerk or schoolteacher.

NOTES

1 J.S. Herbert in the *Church Missionary Society Report* for 1910-11.
2 J.A. Massam, *The Cliff Dwellers of Kenya*, London, Seeley, 1927, p. 8.
3 In Nandi *Mami tie ne makituni.*
4 In Nandi *kipsongoinik* (sing. *kipsongoiya*).
5 A.C. Hollis, *The Nandi*, p. 64.
6 In Nandi *chepkutwa.*
7 In Nandi *tiliet.*
8 On the subject of relationship see: A.C. Hollis, op. cit., pp. 92-4; C.W.B. Huntingford, *The Southern Nilo-Hamites*, pp. 24-5; G.S. Snell, *Nandi Customary Law*, pp. 14-15; F.J. Mumford, *Nandi Studies*

(Revised), Kapsabet, 1959, p. 36, and dictionaries in use at the Africa Inland Church, Kapsabet.

9   J.G. Peristiany, *The Social Institutions of the Kipsigis*, London, 1939, pp. 93-116; B.E. Kipkorir with F.B. Welbourn, *The Marakwet of Kenya*, pp. 6-8, 49-50.

10 Cf. A.C. Hollis, op. cit., p. 94 and G.W.B. Huntingford, loc. cit.

11 In Nandi *oret* (pl. *ortinwek*), literally meaning 'path', 'road', 'line' and derivatively 'clan'.

12 Cf. G.S. Snell, op. cit., pp. 32-3, for a description of the type of punishment meted out on such occasions and quoted in my 'Ritual Change among the Nandi', p. 208.

13 'If a girl became pregnant the child was put into mud and left to die.' (A.J. at Kobujoi, June 1973.) 'If by chance one of these unmarried girls has a child by a warrior during this intercourse, she strangles it as soon as it is born. In such a case the young man who is the father of the child must present the girl with a goat.' (H.H. Johnston, *The Uganda Protectorate*, Vol. II, London, 1902, p. 878.) 'Children are always strangled by the mother, and buried, and the elmoran who is the father presents the ditto with a goat and her father with another goat.' (C.W. Hobley, *Eastern Uganda*, London, 1902, p. 38.)

14 She was called *chesorbuchot* or *kiburon*.

15 In Nandi the *Toiyoi* clan. Cf. A.C. Hollis, op. cit., p. 9 for details.

16 *Njogetab chebiosok* or 'punishment of the woman' meted out to male offenders as described by G.S. Snell, loc. cit.

17 Ibid.

18 G.W.B. Huntingford, *The Southern Nilo-Hamites*, p. 29.

19 K.C. at Kapsabet, 17 October 1973.

20 On this point I am accepting the authority of G.S. Snell (p. 34 of his *Nandi Customary Law*). I am not, however, convinced, as I was told on several occasions that the eldest brother took the responsibility and I note that H.H. Johnston, writing in 1902 (op. cit., p. 42), was of the same opinion: 'When a man dies his eldest brother takes all his wives and property, but the arms of the deceased go to the eldest son.'

21 Cf. for example the views of Paul Kalanda cited in Benezeri Kisembo, Laurenti Magesa and Aylward Shorter, *African Christian Marriage*, London, 1977, pp. 78-80. See also A.R. Radcliffe-Brown's definition of the levirate in A.R. Radcliffe-Brown and Daryll Forde (eds), *African Systems of Kinship and Marriage*, London, 1950, p. 64.

22 In Nandi *kilal mat ab oret*.

23 G.S. Snell relates how the younger woman was impregnated probably by a 'cicisbeo of the deceased's clan'. I was unable to verify this or get any measure of agreement as to the identity of the genitor. Opinions varied between members of the deceased's clan or even *tiliet* (kindred group) and those of the older woman's clan or kindred group. Often, my informants added 'if possible' and so I conclude that at least at present there is no rigid ruling on the matter. See also J.G. Peristiany on a similar custom among the Kipsigis (op. cit., pp. 81-3 and quoted in my 'Ritual Change among the Nandi', pp. 241-3). Aylward Shorter mentions the same custom among the Simbiti of Tanzania and Evans-Pritchard a version called 'ghost marriage' among the Nuer of the Southern Sudan.

(Shorter, CROMIA Circulars, and Evans-Pritchard, *Kinship and Marriage among the Nuer*, Oxford, 1951, p. 111.)

24 In Nandi *kitunchi go*, meaning 'to be married into the house'.

25 M.T. and R.T. and others at Moiben in January 1974.

26 In Nandi *kanyiok* and *tugab chepto* respectively.

27 E.J.M. at Lessos in October 1973.

28 The Nandi terms are: from the suitor *tetab luget*, from his father's sister *tetab senge*, from one of his father's sisters already a mother *tetab lakwet* ...

29 In Nandi *asoya*.

30 In Nandi *katunisiet*.

31 In Nandi *kilda* from the verb *il*, meaning 'to anoint'. Some informants gave *kaildaet*, derived from the same root. The association is the same: 'anointing' when giving the bride in marriage. The journey is the actual 'giving'.

32 In Nandi *boiyob tum* or *boiyot ab katunisiet*.

33 In Nandi respectively *cheplakwet* and *mestowot*.

34 Or 'house of *tumdo*' — in Nandi *gotab tumdo* with the literal meaning of 'house of the ceremony'.

35 Among the Kipsigis, according to Peristiany, the bridal party comprising a warrior, a young boy and girl and the bride are anointed by the girl's parents before leaving on their journey for the bridegroom's home. This 'anointing' may be reflected in the Nandi use of the word *kilda* or *kaildaet* to signify the giving of the bride. I have not been able to trace an actual 'anointing' at this point among the Nandi at present; there are hints, however, that it may have taken place in the past. (Peristiany, op. cit., p. 60.)

36 In Nandi *chepkauiyet* and *kiboet* respectively.

37 The small bell is called *cheptingiliet* and the belt *legetiet*.

38 Cf. A.C. Hollis, op. cit., pp. 61-2; refinements only have changed since then.

39 In Nandi also *katunisiet*, from the verb *tun*, meaning 'to marry'.

40 In Keiyo the *muguriot* ring — B.K. and others in Keiyo during June 1973.

41 B.E. Kipkorir with F.B. Welbourn, op. cit., p. 51; see also pp. 49-53 on Keiyo marriage generally.

42 See J.G. Peristiany, op. cit., pp. 56-75 and I.Q. Orchardson, *The Kipsigis*, Nairobi, 1961, pp. 73-82, on Kipsigis marriage.

43 It is therefore interesting to note that Orchardson, in commenting on Kipsigis marriage, hints that *katunisiet* may have been the main marriage ritual in days gone by:

Though the *Katunisiet* is not essential but only confirmatory, it is regarded as an important social occasion as it entails the entertainment of a very large number of guests for four days. The word is derived from the verb stem *tun*, 'marry', and it may once have been the chief marriage ceremony. The betrothal, or tying, is the ceremony that makes the marriage binding and the *Katunisiet* may be dispensed with by those who cannot afford the expense, without the marriage being prejudiced in any way. It cannot be held until the whole of the marriage cattle have been handed over and found to be satisfactory. It may be postponed for many years until it can be performed together with the third ceremony, *Ewor*. There is a growing tendency to postpone it on account of the cost and the great amount of work it puts upon the women. The ceremony is almost exactly a repetition of the first marriage ceremony including a second tying of the *segutiet* bracelet. *Ewor(ga)*, *Ketebi ngecheret* and *Sonaiek*, the remaining ceremonies connected with marriage, take place in stages later in life. *Sonaiek* is held properly only in old age. (Op. cit., p. 76.)

The second tying of the ritual grass is certainly anomalous; Nandi today, very conscious of the anomaly, try to explain it by affirming that the first tying at betrothal is not original to Nandi but has been borrowed from the Kipsigis or resorted to as a means of ensuring that the girl will be married to the man to whom she has been promised during the engagement visit. If Fr Kuhn of the Mill Hill Mission is to be believed then the binding nature of the ritual grass has declined even in the last forty years: 'In one case I had a difficulty in church. The banns were read three times and then a fellow came up and said "You're marrying my wife to somebody else tomorrow ... " I sent out a message ... The couple came ... "Yes, that's true, I was tied by *segutiet*, but the dowry [sic] was not paid ... " said the woman. I called the chief, a friend of mine. "Look here" I said, "I took it from you when I called you in that *segutiet* was the sign of marriage." "That was in the old days," he replied, "but it's no longer like that now." That was fifteen years ago. I was very sorry to hear it.'

Traditionally, Nandi have intermarried with their Kipsigis, Terik, Keiyo and other Kalenjin neighbours. Moreover, nowadays, apart from many Nandi clans who are reportedly of Kipsigis, Keiyo and Maasai 'blood', there are many members of these groups in Nandi itself; particularly, as I have remarked earlier, there are many Kipsigis 'settlers' in South and central Nandi and there is also a considerable interaction between Nandi and Keiyo in former European settlement areas to the north. This means that in the marriage ritual there has been much borrowing and at times fusion of details. Geographically, the Nandi are placed in the most likely position for interaction and cultural borrowing. Nevertheless, it is still possible to abstract what is essentially Nandi from the varied and often confused accounts — bearing in mind constantly, of course, that it is possible that in the distant past all these peoples shared a common heritage.

44   This particular gourd is known in Nandi as *tareget*.
45   In Nandi *sambut*.
46   According to some informants the bridegroom also wears *chepkejiryet* (a full length sheepskin or goatskin of uniform colour, worn from the shoulders) and *munyawek* (ankle bells).
47   *Sinendet* creeper, the *chepkosinet* gourd and the *sosiot* stick.
48   The sheep is called *chepsegutiet*.
49   The gourd is *mwendet* and the Nandi word for expectorates *kosuut*.
50   This information was given me by an informant who likened the boat going over to the opposite bank of a river to the wife's joining her husband's clan.
51   See Sarah Cherotich, 'The Nandi Female Initiation and Marriage', loc. cit., p. 75.

'Before they are taken in there is a *korosiot* which they surround out-side. Then they go in. Inside they start singing marriage songs. The small girl is to put on her back the calabash. This is a sign of children. And the boy is to be the one looking after cattle.' (Kapsabet schoolgirl, June 1973.) Cf. the 'enacted' or 'prophetic' symbolism of the Old Testament prophets.

52 In Nandi *rogoriosiek.*
53 Cf. A.C. Hollis, op. cit., p. 62. I append two accounts of the ritual intercourse:
    After this, they are told, 'Go and sleep'. They are now called 'You family' because they have been joined. This point of the wedding ceremony is very important and all present as witnesses just look on while the man and the woman perform everything. After this, it is not easy to break off marriage until a divorce ceremony is performed to nullify the marriage. (Sarah Cherotich, loc. cit.)

After this part of the ceremony is completed, the parents of the bride and bridegroom would be motioned to go out of the room. Then, both the bride and the groom would be instructed to play sex. The attendants would prove the man's manhood and the woman's womanhood ... at this point some detail is gone into. (K.C. at Kapkangani in June 1973.)

I have also found some supporting evidence for Sarah Cherotich's description of the first night spent alone together by the bride and groom, and so I quote her account:

The newly weds go to the husband's house. They are escorted and the girl is warned not to yield to the man. If she has not been yielding to men all along, why should she yield to this one now. The man on the other hand is told by the other men not to be defeated unless he is impotent. Each now is determined to do the best, and not to yield to the other. In the house, they are left and they sleep on a new, black smooth skin. This kind of skin is used in wedding ceremonies because other colours would show dirt, and black colour hides it.

The battle follows and the girl is determined not to have anything to do with the man although her husband — the exhortation she got from the women is enough. The man also wants to prove his manhood and so he must get the woman. The man threatens the girl upon refusal but she does not care. They even resort to physical force and the man at this point is forced to ask the question, 'Do you deny me what is rightly mine? I will force you unless you are not yet aware that you are my wife.' He forces her but she wards off any attack because she is strong and bulky since she has been fed well and the man is on his guard. They wrestle and at last the man wins. I do not know if there are cases where the man does not win, but the girl is always told to yield in the end by the women but not give herself away at his first asking. (Sarah Cherotich, loc. cit., pp. 75-6.)

54 In Nandi *sanget.*
55 A.C. Hollis, op. cit., pp. 62-3.
56 Ibid., pp. 63-4.
57 In Nandi the verb *keteitei* is used.
58 The ox-horn is *lalet* and the pot *teret.*

59 In Nandi *kenduiywet* and *senetwet* respectively.

60 *Muganget* of the *tebeng'wet* tree.

61 In Nandi the *sanget* pot.

62 *Kerebet* and *muitab kok* respectively.

63 The wooden knife is called *segetiet*.

64 The words spoken are '*Myonei lakwaa*'.

65 The son-in-law is *sandana* and the first instalment is known as *chebager*. ·

66 In Nandi '*Machie kook injor ka lakwet*'.

67 These were brought to my attention by H.O. Anyumba, responsible for the research project on Music and Dance being undertaken under the auspices of Nairobi University. He recalled particularly a Luo song concerning the long slender necks of Nandi women.

68 All non-Africans were categorised in a blanket manner 'whites' or *wazungu* (Swahili) or *chumbek* (the Nandi for 'strangers', persons wearing clothes, especially Arabs and Europeans).

69 A.T. Matson, *Nandi Resistance*, p. 47.

70 F.J. Jackson, *Early Days in East Africa*, London, 1930, p. 325 (ch. on 'The Railway and the Indians').

71 R. Meinertzhagen, *Kenya Diary: 1902-6*, Edinburgh, 1957, p. 47.

72 *Handbook of Kenya Colony and Protectorate*, London, 1920, p. 340.

73 Nyanza Province, Provincial Commissioner's Report for twelve months ending 31 March 1912 (DC/NDI/1/1).

74 See my 'Ritual Change among the Nandi', p. 247, n. 49, for details.

75 J.E. at Kapsabet Hospital in April 1969: 'Old dressers try to treat VD going around privately — they achieve little, rather leave the disease. There is danger in private treatment.' (Most probably he was referring to 'Jimmy'.)

76 A.T. Matson, op. cit., pp. 25, 29. Often the mistreatment of women on such expeditions led to the breaking of the truce. Cf. A.C. Hollis, op. cit., p. 17: 'When food is scarce in the land ... women have to undertake long journeys to purchase what is required.'

77 Alice Gold, 'The Economic Role of the Nandi Woman in the 19th and 20th Centuries', p. 7. I have been in correspondence with Alice Gold of the University of California, Los Angeles, and she observes: 'The period of Nandi resistance to the British, 1895-1906, introduced a new shift towards agriculture and a broadening of female economic activities and responsibilities which temporarily took up the slack left by the temporary loss of Nandi male economic roles.' (Op. cit., p. 6.) She quotes Stigand on p. 7.

78 Alice Gold, loc. cit., p. 7 where she bases her conclusions on the findings of Huntingford in his *Nandi Work and Culture*, London, 1950, p. 65, q.v.

79 Dated 26 February 1936 and included in ARs 1933-47 (DC/NDI/1/4):

The question I propounded to myself was why the Nandi provide the greatest no. of prostitutes — proportion to the numbers, of any tribe in Kenya. (I am assuming this as a fact; I have never heard it disputed.) These prostitutes come from 2 sources — unmarried girls and young wives (some not so young!). As regards the first class, these are undoubtedly sent out as a rule, by the male relatives — father, uncle, brother — to 'spoil the Egyptians' ... I regret to say that I believe a considerable part of the Nandi Hut and Poll Tax is paid from this source. It saves the male taxpayers having to work for wages or dispose of stock. As regards the second class, wives, these are runaways, and the only reason I have ever been able to find for their running away, is because their husbands beat them. Nandi husbands and wives do not love each other in the way we regard as usual; any such emotion is got over before the parties come to marriage, in the promiscuous sexual life of the 'moran' and the 'ndito'. Marriage is apparently purely a material affair, and the husband is ready to beat his wife for the slightest shortcoming, usually when he is drunk. If the wife has no children, she then takes herself off and goes to the nearest settled area as a prostitute, or to live with a succession of men whom she fancies.

It may still be asked, however, why Nandi women take to prostitution so easily. I am informed they did not do so before the Nandi War of 1906. There is word that a great many young Nandi women were debauched by the askaris [soldiers] of that time and that this opened up a new vista to them. I believe that their predisposition to prostitution arises from the traditional promiscuity when adolescent, coupled with the provision of opportunity at their doors — namely the settled areas of Trans-Nzoia, Uasin Gishu and Kisumu-Londiani, and the even richer ground of the Kakamega Gold Fields, which are full of various wage-earning natives with no women of their own. A Nandi woman who wishes to get some money, either for her family or for herself, must go outside Nandi for it, as prostitution — that is, with the element of payment — is practically unknown in Nandi itself.

Success in the profession has given rise to tradition in the matter, and hence the position today. It is interesting to note that the Lumbwa sisters of the Nandi are also noted for a propensity to prostitution, but to a definitely lesser extent than the Nandi, no doubt because of the more unfavourable situation; while other akin pastoral tribes provide very few prostitutes, as they practically entirely lack the opportunities of contact which the Nandi have. As an illustration of how this works, I may say there is no point in the Nandi Reserve where a person is more than some two hours reach from another District.

80 Personal knowledge gained from visiting families in Kapsabet and Kaptumo.

81 Philip and Geraldine McMinn (AIM missionaries) at Kapsabet in October 1973, and others.

82 'Although generalization it would appear that the annual marriage rate in a society is likely to approximate to some 8 marriages per thousand of the population.' See 'Statistics Relating to the Frequency of Marriage in Church', Appendix E, pp. 134-53, of Adrian Hastings, *Christian Marriage in Africa*, London, 1973, for a full discussion of the subject.

83 Personal examination of marriage records. The AIC (Africa Inland Church) figure is for the whole of the District, the Catholic figure is that of the largest parish, Chepterit. The civil marriages for the same period numbered sixteen in 1969 (including one European) and twenty-nine in 1970 (including a European/Nandi wedding and also including the marriage of five members of the Full Gospel Church, Nandi Hills).

84 Cf. A.T. Matson, op. cit., p. 13; his figures are based on administrative records.

85 This latter point was made to me by a group of people when discussing the issue and they referred particularly to Nandi being willing to have smaller families than produce children who might be compelled for economic reasons to become labourers and house servants like the Luyia.

VII. Divorce

Of all the Kalenjin peoples the Nandi possessed the most developed divorce ritual. When, for example, we examine the Pokot at one extreme and the Kipsigis at another we find that the Pokot, although allowing divorce in rare instances on grounds of barrenness, did not possess a ritual with which to formalise it, while the Kipsigis put divorcees through a ritual similar to although decidedly simpler than that of the Nandi.

Two things need to be said about the literature on the subject. First, all writers on Kalenjin customary law since and including Hollis, for example Snell and Huntingford on the Nandi, Peristiany and Orchardson on the Kipsigis and Kipkorir and Welbourn on the Marakwet, apparently describe the practice at the time of writing. Secondly, the writers on the Nandi at least appear to make little or no allowance for differences due to various springs of origin be they clan, ethnic or geographical.

For these reasons and also because the changes which have taken place in Nandi divorce ritual over the past fifty years are considerable, I adopt in this chapter a different manner of approach: I set down first (so far as they are possible to ascertain) the traditional Nandi law and ritual of divorce as they were practised at the beginning of the century, taking into account variations in practice arising from clan and ethnic differences; I then seek to enumerate and elucidate the changes in thinking and practice brought about by the coming of the missionaries and the onset of colonial government. And finally, I describe the facts as I find them in the 1950s, 1960s and 1970s.

1. *Traditional Divorce: 'To rend the bag'*[1]

The Nandi believed marriage to be in principle indissoluble. This belief had two practical consequences (or vice versa, the belief reflected the practices). One was the denial or remarriage to widows, the other was the withholding of divorce in any absolute sense from any except childless couples who had become totally incompatible.

With regard to widows it is important to realise that there was no need for a Nandi widow to remarry: she could be cared for (after the leviratic custom) by her late husband's brother, or become party to marriage with a younger woman, although she could not be compelled to do either. Similarly, a Nandi man whose wife was barren had no need to divorce her: provided he was able to afford the bridewealth he could always take a second wife, or, if very old, allow his wife to resort to the expediency of woman marriage, and so 'relight the fire of the clan'.

(i) *Grounds for Divorce*

In the accounts of A.C. Hollis,[2] G.W.B. Huntingford[3] and G.S. Snell[4] on divorce among the Nandi I have found a great deal of uncertainty and confusion particularly concerning the grounds for divorce and the distinction between 'divorce' and 'separation'. On those points I am not convinced that the writers were certain of their facts. Consequently I have based my account of the ritual and conclusions concerning the grounds for and nature of divorce on the authority of Nandi elders belonging to the *Nyongi* and *Maina* age-sets.

There was only one form of absolute divorce among the Nandi. Called *kebet lol*, meaning 'to rend the bag', it involved taking an oath of divorce and was rare.[5] Many to whom I spoke had never witnessed the ceremony. Only a childless couple could go through the ritual. Yet childlessness in itself was not considered adequate grounds for divorce, there had to be indications of irretrievable breakdown or evidence of other exceptional circumstances.[6]

Conditions regarded as indicating irretrievable breakdown were repeated acts of adultery, refusal of conjugal rights, continuous quarrelsomeness, incompatibility of husband and wife, and conviction of the wife for sorcery.

Exceptional circumstances in which divorce might be permitted were twofold: (1) if it emerged that a couple had married within the prohibited degrees of clan or kindred group either deliberately or unwittingly then the clan elders could seek a divorce (when children had already been born of the union objections were considered to have been overruled); (2) if murder occurred between members of the husband's and wife's respective clans divorce could be applied for.

Allow me to repeat, if the couple had children, none of these reasons was considered as adequate justification for seeking divorce.

The varying practices relating to separation (to be discussed later) I regard as different attempts to accord some kind of recognition to separation of spouses customarily prevented from obtaining a divorce.

(ii) *Procedures for Divorce*

It was not very difficult for adequate grounds for divorce to develop between the spouses in a childless marriage. Particularly, if the wife was a husband's first and only wife he might well become quarrelsome in the face of continuing infertility. Then he might advance reasons for his tragic state. Perhaps it was due to adultery, or maybe sorcery or possibly it was because the marriage had been within the prohibited degrees. These were areas for investigation. And if the husband was poor and could not afford a second wife then all the more reason why he should seek to obtain a divorce, and, with the returned bride-wealth, marry again.

After due consideration he approached the elders of neighbourhood and clan declaring his intention to seek divorce from his wife. Relatives of both parties were summoned and efforts made at reconciliation of the couple. These efforts were often great because of bridewealth considerations and ties of kinship. As one of my informants said:

The divorce does not occur due to communal concern but from both partners ... The elders determine and dig out why these people want to divorce one another. Perhaps a simple matter or a quarrel made them dislike one another so that the elders try any possible way of bringing them to understanding and make them love as before, forgetting about the past. They may do this many times trying to mend any quarrel that arises. But finally if they are defeated they decide what to do. They ask whether one or the other wants to part and live independently. ... Divorce does not come into effect unless both declare their agreement and unless full information is obtained by the elders.

In the past, divorce was held in a similar way to any other ceremony performed. People were called on a day fixed for the rite, to witness that Mr and Mrs So-and-so had left one another for life. From thence, neither of them calls the other husband or wife. The elders of the clan to which these members belong are to organize the situation. Before they perform [the rite] they have to call for two special and big meetings in which the two are accused. The reason for this is to persuade the couple to change their minds or for one to refuse to leave the other. If they find both still lamenting [about their grievances] and affirming hatred of the other then another day is fixed for the uncovering of the truth and falsity of the various accusations.[7]

The husband alone, not the wife, could initiate divorce proceedings among the Nandi. A woman could not go to the neighbourhood elders and ask to divorce her husband. On the other hand, she could do a great deal to compel either her husband or relatives to seek a dissolution of the marriage. Sorcery aside, a Nandi woman was most frequently accused by her husband of failure to give him respect, and laziness in the preparation and cooking of his food. Beating was a matter of routine discipline as evidenced in the advice given by a father when enquiring after his daughters whom he had left in the care of Colonel R. Meinertzhagen: 'No woman could ever keep out of mischief if she was not soundly beaten every few days.'[8] When through drunkenness or rage a man's beating became intolerable his wife ran first to his age-mates for protection or redress and then to her own family for refuge.[9] If the situation proved irretrievable, relatives had to make some efforts to come to terms with the problem, probably by allowing divorce proceedings to go ahead.

(iii) *Rites of Divorce*

When elders and relatives decided that divorce was inevitable in a given situation, the master of ceremonies who presided at the couple's wedding ceremony was sought out, together with elders or neighbourhood and clan and immediate relatives.[10] If the original wedding elder was not available — he might have already died — then a suitable elder of the same generation was asked to take his place. The day was then set for the divorce rites to be performed.

The couple was expected to come with a newly-sewn bag made either of leather (if possible from the skin of the animal slaughtered at the wedding ceremony) or from the plant *sedum* species, the stalk of which had been hollowed by the removal of its pith.[11] The leather bag was about the width of a man's hand — 4 inches across — and about 6 inches in depth; the fibrous bag was probably much smaller. In either case, the bag was filled with fine soil and could be sewn or left open at the top. It could be brought to the assembly by either of the partners but I am told that it was most likely brought by the wife 'to show her determination in the matter'.[12] Before the ritual began, the elders, for the last time, sought to effect reconciliation by probing further into the attitudes of the parties to the divorce.

Failing reconciliation, the master of ceremonies placed all in attendance in order, and commenced the ritual proper. He formally asked the couple if they were intent on divorce and issued warnings concerning the seriousness and consequences of what they were about to do. They were, he would point out, about to call one another by names considered inappropriate within the marriage relationship and after that there would be no going back.[13]

The couple, facing one another, then took hold of the bag between them, and prepared to pull it apart or have it cut by the presiding elder, after taking the oath of divorce. The essence of the oath was the calling by each partner of the other by the 'porridge name' given at birth and not used by a person during married life, especially if addressing one's spouse.[14] This symbolised the severing of the husband-wife relationship and the dialogue in two parts went as follows:

		1.
HUSBAND:	*'Chebiwot!'*	(husband calls out wife's name)
WIFE:	*'Yiw!'*	(wife responds)
HUSBAND:	*'Tapkwenya!'*	(greeting to girl)
WIFE:	*'Igoo!'*	(wife responds)
HUSBAND:	*'Maamochin.'*	('I am no longer with you.')

		2.
WIFE:	*'Kipkemei!'*	(wife calls out husband's name)
HUSBAND:	*'Wou!'*	(husband responds)
WIFE:	*'Subai!'*	(greeting to boy)
HUSBAND:	*'Ebo!'*	(husband responds)
WIFE:	*'Maamochin.'*	('I am no longer with you.')[15]

Whereupon the bag was torn or cut.[16] As the soil fell to the ground, the wife swore words to this effect: 'If I will ever come into this house, this soil eat me!' Likewise, the husband took an oath: 'If I will ever say you are mine, this soil eat me!'[17] Alternatively, the elder administered the oath and the parties assented. The couple then turned their backs on one another without looking and were forbidden for the remainder of the day to greet one another. Afterwards, they were permitted to greet in terms of friendship and respect but not of intimacy.

The bridewealth was returned and any children which might be born to the woman in after years could not be claimed by her former husband.[18]

2. *Government and Mission Innovations*

From the onset of British rule in Nandi in 1896 and the coming of the first missionaries in 1909 the Nandi were faced with two serious threats to the stability of their marriage structures. The former, as we have seen in the last chapter, brought new influences which led to an increase in sexual promiscuity; the latter, rather less obviously, brought new beliefs, particularly concerning the status of women, which led among other things to the encouragement of divorce and remarriage of widows among the Nandi. A few examples of legislation and practice will suffice to make the point.

(i) *The Marriage Acts (Ordinances)*

The statute law of Kenya came into being with the East Africa Order in Council which, in 1897, applied certain British and Indian Acts to the East Africa Protectorate. The Order (of 1902) provided that:

In all cases, civil and criminal, to which natives are parties, every Court shall be guided by native law so far as it is applicable and is not repugnant to justice and morality or inconsistent with any Order in Council or Ordinance, or any regulation or rule made under any Order in Council or Ordinance; and shall decide all such cases according to substantial justice without undue regard to technicalities of procedure and without undue delay.[19]

and gave Her Majesty's Commissioner power to make Ordinances, subject to the qualification that in so doing

The Commissioner shall respect existing native laws and customs except so far as the same may be opposed to justice or morality.[20]

In the same year the Commissioner exercised this power with the enactment of the Marriage Act, still in force in Kenya today, somewhat amended but substantially the same.[21] The Act provided for Christian (although the word was not used) and civil marriages, monogamous in form. Customary marriages were recognised and the existence of a customary marriage was made an impediment to statutory marriage with any other person. Moreover, it became an offence for a person married under customary law to contract a marriage under the Act or for a person married under the Act to contract a marriage under customary law.

Then in 1904 the Native Christian Marriage Ordinance was enacted; this applied only to the marriage of Christian Africans. It was replaced in 1931 by the African Christian Marriage and Divorce Act, applicable to the marriage of Africans when either or both partners professed Christianity but not preventing Africans from contracting marriage in accordance with the Marriage Act. In 1904, also, the Divorce Ordinance was enacted. It was based on the Indian Divorce Act, 1869, and was replaced in 1941 by the Matrimonial Causes Act based on the English Supreme Court of Judicature (Consolidation) Act, 1925, and Matrimonial Causes Act, 1937.

Originally, Islamic law in Kenya applied to the coastal regions only (in the sovereignty of the Sultan of Zanzibar) but in 1906 the Mahommedan Marriage and Divorce Registration Act was enacted, providing for the registration of Muslim marriages. The provisions of this Act were progressively extended by districts until in 1928 the Act applied to all Muslims.

A Government Notice dated 9 May 1905 applied the Marriage Act to Nandi, appointing the District Commissioner Registrar of Marriages and his Assistant Deputy Registrar, for the District.[22] On 15 June 1920 application was made for the appointment of Mahommed bin Salim Badra as *Khadhi* or Registrar of Mahommedan marriages and divorce.[23] Then, on 1 October 1924, a licence was issued to the Africa Inland Mission 'to celebrate marriages at Aldai chapel'.[24]

In this manner the Nandi found in their midst at least three alien marriage laws and rites, two of which allowed monogamous marriage only and all of which permitted divorce on different grounds from those recognised by Nandi customary law. The first Nandi marriages under the Act took place, so far as I can ascertain, at Namgoi near Kapsabet, in 1926.[25] From the beginning, the missionaries allowed marriage of widows and encouraged civil divorce so as to make way for marriages between Christians in church. As we have already noted, this was partly due to their opposition to female circumcision and partly to their concern for the plight of women in Nandi society.

(ii) *African Courts*

From the consolidation of British rule until 1967 Kenya was without a unified judicial system. For a time three different systems operated side by side — one for Africans, one for non-Africans and one for Muslims.

In Nandi, as we have seen, questions concerning marriage and divorce were traditionally dealt with by the neighbourhood elder, who was upheld by public opinion and assisted by the warriors. However, from the inception of colonial administrative and judicial procedures the course of Nandi customary law was set in the direction of change. At first, the change was relatively imperceptible, particularly with regard to marriage and divorce, but latterly it has become increasingly apparent.

First among the administrative changes was the division of the newly-constituted Reserve into twenty-five locations in 1907. Then came the implementation of the Local Native Authority Ordinance of 1924, setting up Local Native Councils in each District. Alongside the Council in Nandi there was erected a judicial structure of magistrates' and headmen's courts.[26] These latter were for Africans and were resorted to when the neighbourhood council of elders was unable satisfactorily to resolve problems. They brought a new distinction to Nandi, the distinction between civil and criminal offences. In 1926, for example, three civil cases were heard. There was no appeal other than to the District Commissioner.

In 1931, a new system came into force with the enactment of the Native Tribunals Ordinance, 1930. The role of the courts was taken over by the newly-constituted Native Tribunals which were much more formal in character. At the same time the number of locations was reduced to nine and a Tribunal appointed for each. Each tribunal had five members — an appointed president and four elected members — plus a clerk. Official headmen did not sit on these tribunals. Offences tried included criminal cases of assault and breaches of headmen's orders and civil cases of stock and marriage disputes, the latter being the commonest. Of these tribunals G.W.B. Huntingford wrote in 1953:

The most important change brought about by British administration is that the *kokuet* now has less power than formerly ... The introduction of a system of tribunals for legal purposes, and of a Local Native Council as a public authority, is having a considerable effect on the native institutions, and though neither have links with any existing tribal institution, they are now beginning when the authority of the elders is weakening, to take the place of the *kokuet* as a court, though it still functions in a restricted manner.[27]

In 1951, the Local Native Councils became the African District Councils and the Native Tribunals became African Courts.[28] From that year the number of tribunals in Nandi was reduced to five and located at Kabiyet, Kilibwoni, Chemundu, Kaptumo and Serem, with the Appeal Tribunal meeting quarterly at Kapsabet. Within the jurisdiction of these courts came marriage and divorce according to 'native' law and claims for bridewealth or adultery founded on 'native' law.

With the enactment of the Magistrates' Courts Act, 1967, integration of the judicial system was achieved. The new system is three-tiered,

comprising Subordinate (or District Magistrates') Courts, Courts of
Appeal and the High Court. The transfer of power from neighbourhood council to court in Nandi continues to gain momentum with the
courts now issuing 'certificates of divorce'.[29] The final stage will
come with the enactment of the proposed new 'Law of Marriage and
Divorce'.[30]

3. *Contemporary Practices of Divorce and Separation*

(i) *Elders*

It is evident from the foregoing that the authority and power exercised
in the past by Nandi elders has been to a great extent eroded.
Consequently, traditional divorce sanctioned by the elders is very rare
today except in a few areas which for one reason or another have
resisted or to some extent escaped full-scale social change. One such
area is Tindiret on the borders of Kipsigis country. There Nandi
couples go through a divorce ritual influenced by Kipsigis custom. My
informants believed that the people had borrowed from the Kipsigis
in recent years, replacing 'rending the bag' with a ritual of 'anointing'.[31]

As for the ritual itself — 'anointing' — it is uncomplicated. As with
'rending the bag' the couple to be divorced must be childless and the
bridewealth must be returned. The elders bring clarified butter in a
ritual ox-horn. As the man first calls out the woman's porridge name
he anoints her; she then calls him by his porridge name and anoints
him. Afterwards they go their own separate ways.

No reason was offered for the change, or explanation given of the
ritual's symbolism.[32]

(ii) *Courts*

Claims for divorce, claims concerning conjugal rights, claims for return
of bridewealth and custody of children regularly come before the
Subordinate and Appeal Courts nowadays. In 1955 the court at Serem
dealt with eight cases and in 1956 with sixteen cases. In 1957 the court
at Kilibwoni dealt with fifteen cases and in 1958 with nine cases. In
1962 the Court of Appeal at Kapsabet dealt with seven cases and in
1965 with eleven cases. These are figures which I was able to compile
from court records. Yet these cases brought before the courts represent
only a fraction of the marriages affected by breakdown in relationships. However, before we go on to consider breakdown and separation of spouses I should like to give some concrete examples of suits
actually filed for divorce and of the judgments given.[33]
(*a*) On 12 April 1961, an appeal by one Arap Tuwei against a decision
of the Kabiyet Court was made at the Appeal Court Kapsabet.

First, the appellant stated how fifteen years earlier he, a Nandi, had married a Nandi woman, agreeing with her parents to pay a bridewealth of eight cattle. He could only produce four and while trying to obtain the remainder his wife was given by her parents to another man, the respondent. But after several years, his wife returned to him (1960) and the respondent filed a case at Kabiyet which he won. But the woman remained with him, the appellant, and refused to return to the respondent.

Second, the respondent's son stated how his stepmother had stayed with his father for fifteen years and how she had then run away to stay with the appellant who at the beginning had failed to pay the bridewealth.

Third, the respondent, Arap Chumo, stated how he had married the woman, giving eight head of cattle for her. She had remained with him fifteen years during which time she had borne him two children.

Finally, the verdict declared:

1. The woman being disputed by both parties was first married by Nandi customary law to the appellant.

2. Because he was unable to pay the bridewealth agreed on, the girl's parents married her to another man, the respondent, who paid a bridewealth of eight head of cattle.

3. The woman stayed with the respondent for about fourteen years during which time she bore him two daughters.

4. After fourteen years she went back to the appellant.

5. The respondent who is a *Nyongi* and very old has stated that he and his wife cannot live together any longer because she is very young.

6. The woman has stated in court that she and her husband will no longer stay in the same house.

7. The old man insists that the children are his.

8. Therefore, the court awards the respondent fourteen head of cattle for his two daughters. The woman is to stay with the appellant who is to become father to her two daughters.[34]

Several points may be noted from this case. Strictly speaking, according to customary law, the appellant was the woman's legal husband and he was the legal or social father of her two children. But the question of bridewealth paid by the respondent had obviously complicated the issue. The judgment lays a great deal of emphasis on the wishes and circumstances of the people concerned, rather than on the letter of the law. The latter is a tendency which we shall observe again in the cases to follow.

(*b*) In a case heard at Kabiyet Appeal Court on 9 December 1959 and 25 March 1960, the couple concerned agreed to divorce.

The woman alleged that she (the appellant, original defendant) had been sent away by her husband when he married a second wife. She complained of his ill-treatment and that she had had no children by him. He agreed to file a divorce case at Kilibwoni but failed to turn up and threatened to kill her later. When, later, the case did go to court the court ordered them to remain together. The husband alleged that his wife had run away from him before his second marriage. He had followed her to Elgeyo whereupon she stated she was a Christian. He refused to allow her to go to church and when she ran away again he beat her. The appellant's father said he had nothing to say, as his daughter did not complain about her husband while staying with him; it was up to the court to decide. Her mother, on the other hand, stated that the respondent had been going to her demanding the return of the bridewealth.

The court then adjourned and when it met again the appellant explained how the respondent had gone alone (not as agreed) and driven away the cattle from her parents' home, saying at the same time that he did not want her as his wife. The respondent in reply alleged that the appellant did not turn up at the neighbourhood council meeting as arranged, rather, when he went to her home she chased him away with a matchet. So he did not consider her his wife any longer and took away the cattle due to him.

The findings stated that both agreed on divorce. The woman had threatened her husband with a matchet after staying away from him for four years and having a child by another man.[35]

Points to be noted in this case are that the woman initiated the appeal and divorce was granted both because each of the partners wished it and because the court was satisfied that there was adequate evidence of marital breakdown.

(*c*) On 17 April 1957 a husband filed a suit at Chemundu, claiming that he had married his wife in 1940 but that shortly afterwards she had gone to Eldoret and thence to Nairobi.

After some years he had sent his brother to fetch her and her children from Nairobi because he was afraid that when he became old the children might be brought back to him and his cattle sold. Now, as she had been away for seventeen years and none of her children was his, he wanted a divorce. Replying, the defendant stated that after her marriage the plaintiff started 'fighting' with her when his first wife returned from circumcision.[36] She became ill and stayed with her mother for a short time returning to her husband later. But again he ill-treated her and the other women advised her to leave him. So she went to Nairobi for seven years but had been at her parents' home for ten years and during that time the plaintiff had not tried to fetch her back. The court then told the plaintiff that his wife still wanted him. He replied. 'She has been gone for seventeen years and therefore she is no longer mine.' The court allowed the divorce and the couple 'made their divorce in front of the elders'.[37]

An interesting point to note here is the husband's reason for requesting divorce. Without divorce he was reckoned the legitimate if not the biological father of his wife's children and so they could make claims on him for payment of bridewealth at marriage. He did not wish to lose his cattle in this way.

(*d*) On 9 September 1958 a judgment was given, also at Chemundu, ordering a couple to divorce in front of the elders who were present at the hearing:

Plaintiff: 'I have come here in order that I may divorce my wife because she has troubled me for a long time. Again, while I was in Nairobi I was told that I had been given a wife and when I came home I married her and went with her to Eldoret. But while I was with her she started troubling me and I told her to go home. I remained alone and one day I came to see what had happened. I came home three times but she was absent. I went to the house of defendant's father but I was told that she was here sometimes. I went and found her in the house of X. When I was transferred to KPT she came to Eldoret...

'I now say I don't want my former wife, from now onwards. That is all I have to say.'

Defendant: 'One day when I was married by plaintiff and he was away he wrote a letter to his parents as well as my parents, saying "She doesn't want to marry me". He even refused to come and marry me. One day he fought me and told me "You must go to your father's house without any delay". I thought of going home. I now say that I don't want the plaintiff any more as he said.'

Father of the plaintiff: 'I went and asked the defendant to marry and she agreed. When the wedding was about to take place there was a letter from the plaintiff, and on the way the defendant told me that the plaintiff didn't want her any more.'[38]

A point to note here is the determination of the couple not to live together as man and wife although the marriage had been arranged by their parents and that their determination was rewarded with divorce. (*e*) Two interesting cases involving circumcision were heard, also at Chemundu, in July 1957 and October 1959 respectively. I record the first *verbatim* and the second in summary form:

Plaintiff: 'I was friend of the defendant since the year 1951, but when I got word from him I departed from him. But he persuaded me to marry him... but I refused him. One day he called me to his house but when I reached there he gave me some drinks. When I was drunk he took me and circumcised me unknowingly. But now I say I don't want him any more.'

Defendant: 'What the plaintiff has said, that I have been a friend of the plaintiff since 1951, is true. But one day the plaintiff came and asked me to go and circumcise her but after circumcision she was forced by her parents not to marry me. Well now, if the plaintiff has refused to marry me I don't have anything to say. I can divorce her.'

Witness: 'What I say is that I don't want the defendant to marry my daughter.'

Judgment: 'All elders of the court agreed for their divorce because the plaintiff as well as her parents refused the defendant.'[39]

The divorce was made in front of the elders.

The second case was dismissed. The court disagreed with the plaintiff's claim on his wife for whom he said he had paid 400 shillings in bridewealth because they found that he had circumcised the defendant's daughter without his permission, the defendant already having promised his daughter to another man.[40]

(*f*) Two cases heard at Kabiyet in April 1973 resulted in divorce being awarded *under customary law* by consent of the parties after long periods of separation (nine years and fifteen years respectively).[41]

The significant point again here is the emphasis on consent and the fact that at least one of the parties had already married a second time, years before a divorce was sought.

(g) The most interesting of the cases which I noted was filed during 1972-3 at Kapsabet.

The husband was plaintiff; married in 1964, paying six head of cattle and shs 600/- in cash as bridewealth, he had two children but his wife deserted him during March 1970, returned in October and deserted him again later. This was his case, supported by an advocate: 'Under Nandi custom if a wife leaves her husband without reason, that may cause a divorce. If a marriage is dissolved the husband takes the children. I am entitled to take the custody of the children ... I have six acres of land, my salary is shs 390/-, my second wife has one child and I am able to maintain them all. My firstborn has not started school; if she lived with me she would. After divorce I am not supposed to maintain her [my wife] after my customs. Under the custom if we divorce I am entitled to the return of my dowry [sic]. If I take the children, I may be entitled to four cows. For the two children I will leave two cows and take four cows and shs 400/-. I claim also the costs of this petition.'

In reply the wife made various protestations concerning negligence.

Then the first public witness stated: 'I am a *kokwet* [neighbourhood] elder. If a marriage is dissolved the custody of the children goes with the husband. A divorced wife is not entitled to maintenance. *If a man takes the children he does not take the dowry* [sic] — the number of children is irrelevant under the customs. If the children stay away from the father after divorce he will not maintain them. If a wife deserts the husband for one year at least that does not entitle her to be divorced. If a husband refuses and the wife wants to they can be given a temporary period to live together. If they fail, then the divorce can be granted.'

After some wrangling, the case was adjourned until 29 January 1973. Then the wife's uncle testified: 'In Nandi custom if a man sends away his wife he is not entitled to the return of the dowry [sic]. If he has got a child or two the dowry [sic] cannot be returned. In a case of divorce the children will be taken by the husband.'

Another witness next alleged that the children could be shared and still another that the bridewealth could not be returned, 'I know the parties because we come from the same village. The plaintiff married A. in 1964 and we believe that she is still his wife up to now. We Kalenjin do not ask for dowry [sic] twice ... '

For the plaintiff his lawyer replied: 'I do not want to waste time. You have heard the evidence. Plaintiff claims customary divorce on ground that the first defendant did not obey him when he told her to go home and cultivate. In Nandi, that is enough ground for divorce. In Nandi if a divorce is granted the husband is entitled to the custody of the children. As for dowry [sic] in Nandi customary law, if the husband takes the children no dowry [sic] is refundable. I therefore leave that point for the court to grant. I refer the court to Cotran's Customary Law.'

The wife pleaded against the divorce. The judgment was set forth with a summary of the case and several considerations:

'This case was filed by the plaintiff against the two defendants, namely A. for divorce and her father Arap S. for the return of the dowry [sic]. The plaintiff was represented by a Mr M. the advocate whereas the two defendants were not represented ...

'1. Has desertion been proved? Are there adequate grounds for divorce? If what the witness says is true then A. cannot be accused of deserting. If the husband only went for her once he didn't try hard to get her. Both may be the cause.

'2. In the course of the hearing of this suit Mr M. tended to emphasize some aspects of Nandi customary law as regards the custody of children and the return of the bride price [sic]. I find that it is not necessary to go into these as they are not relevant to my findings. It is a waste of time if grounds for divorce not feasible.

'Therefore, the plaintiff's plea under Nandi customary law must fail. The plaintiff has filed this suit with a view to defeating the ends of justice in that should divorce be granted the maintenance order would naturally abate.'[42]

Points to be noted here are the plaintiff's wanting the 'best of both worlds' — of Nandi customary law and marriage under the Act — and that the magistrate based his judgment on his belief that adequate grounds for divorce were not proven.

(*h*) Finally, I quote two other relevant cases.

The first concerns a claim for a 'legal divorce certificate'.

The plaintiff alleged that in April 1971 she married the defendant and in July 1971 he sent her away and at the same time withdrew the bridewealth from her parents, *making a full divorce under Nandi custom*. Consequently, she asked for a 'legal divorce' *since the marriage was already nullified under customary law*. The defendant wrote a letter asking that the request should not be granted as he had taken only two of the four cattle given in bridewealth. The case was dismissed.[43]

The second allowed the plaintiff to divorce her husband because he had beaten her and chased her away.[44]

(iii) *Couples*

What seems clear is that there has been in Nandi a gradual departure over the past fifty years or so from the practice of 'rending the bag' or any form of judicial separation by the elders as recorded by Hollis and Huntingford.[45] Instead, couples make their own arrangements and when disputes arise go to the courts for divorce. Let me illustrate. There has developed in parts of Nandi District during the present *Sawe* generation's young manhood — within the past fifteen years or so — what we might call the embryo of a new rite of separation.

About 1961, in a place called Itigo in central Nandi, there was a man who wanted to send his wife away.[46] Twice he told her to go and she refused. The third time, as darkness was approaching, he lit a hurricane lamp for her — to show her on her way. Eventually, when she arrived home, it was high noon and to everybody's amazement the lamp was still burning. The strange story went round and I have heard of numerous instances of a husband's either actually giving his wife a lamp or threatening to give her one — meaning that he wished her to depart from him and go home to her parents. Similarly, when people speak of a woman 'taking the cat' or 'taking her possessions' they are referring to her having separated from her husband and having taken her dower with her. In the Tindiret area where 'anointing' has displaced 'rending the bag' the people speak of *koongei* (literally, 'to chase each other') when referring to a form of separation agreed to by the spouses.

So what was formerly a matter of agreement between spouses and sanction by relatives and elders of clan and neighbourhood has become a matter of mutual arrangement between spouses and sometimes their immediate relatives. But disputes may arise concerning custody of children, inheritance, remarriage, and the constitution of a person's kindred group etc.; then the courts are approached for 'legal divorce'. In sum, a corporate rite is being individualised by social change only to find its corporateness eventually restored in the courts.

NOTES

1   In Nandi *kebet lol*. The variant *betetab lol* means 'the rending of the bag'. Both derive from the verb *bet*, 'to tear' or 'to rend'. Derivatively, the same verb *bet* means 'to set free' and *kebet lol* signifies divorce.

2   A.C. Hollis, *The Nandi*, p. 69.

3   G.W.B. Huntingford, *The Southern Nilo-Hamites*, p. 29; *Nandi Work and Culture*, p. 18.

4   G.S. Snell, *Nandi Customary Law*, p. 29.

5   In Nandi *mumiat ab betetab lol*.

6   Elders were adamant on this point. One former chief with the administration, Joel Arap Malel of the *Nyongi* generation, chief for many years of Kosirai location, related how in his seventy-four years he had never witnessed a woman divorced for childlessness.

7   N.K.A.B. at Eldoret in June 1973.

8   R. Meinertzhagen, *Kenya Diary: 1902-6*, p. 232.

9   Cf. A.C. Hollis, op. cit., p. 69.

10   In Nandi the *boiyot ab katunisiet*, literally 'the wedding elder'.

11   In Nandi *kuserwet*. Abdul Kadir Limo Arap Korir, of the *Maina* age-set, at Kapsabet, on 12 November 1973, and others informed me that Nandi with Maasai connections used the leather bag and those with Kipsigis, Keiyo and Terik connections the *kuserwet* plant. Arap Korir himself belonged to the *Kabil* clan and claimed Maasai connections.

12   N.K.A.B. at Eldoret in June 1973.

13 The expression used by my informant was 'non-husband' and 'non-wife'.

14 In Nandi *kemaik ab musarek.*

15 G.M.C. at Chemuswo in June 1973.

16 The elder cut the bag with a traditional knife called a *royetab chok* or with a *panga* (Swahili for broad-bladed knife like matchet) since its introduction to Nandi.

17 In Nandi *'Ngot ko tatun anyo goi, koama kugunyechu!'* and *'Ngot ko tatun ale i nenyu koama kugunyechu!'* respectively.

18 A.C. Hollis, followed by G.W.B. Huntingford, seems to claim otherwise, viz. that the bridewealth was not returned unless the husband could find another man to marry his former wife. I have found no precedent for this. It is best explained as a particular arrangement between two kindred groups. G.S. Snell (op. cit., p. 30) also appears convinced that there was a procedure by which the effect of *kebet lol* could be cancelled: 'The parties took a stalk of the kuserwet, which was anointed with fat by a member of a senior age-grade, who also smeared fat upon the arms of the parties and expectorated beer over them as a token of blessing, symbolically bidding the kuserwet stalk to be at rest and inoperative. As far as possible the same animals, or, failing that, animals of the same description, were transferred again to the woman's family and the marriage was thereby revalidated without a repetition of the marriage rite.' I was unable to confirm this.

19 The East Africa Order in Council, 1902, Article 20.

20 Ibid., Article 12 (3).

21 All Ordinances subsisting on 12 December 1963 were restyled Acts by L.N. 2 of 1964.

22 Government Notice No. 165 dated 9 May 1905 and signed 'B. Stone'. (DC/NDI/3/2.)

23 AR for 1919-20 contains a letter dated 15 June 1920 making the application under Section 4 of Ordinance No. 13 of 1906. (DC/NDI/1/2.)

24 'Marriage Ordinance. A licence has been issued to Africa Inland Mission to celebrate marriage at Aldai chapel under Government Notice No. 315 of 1/10/'24.' (DC/NDI/3/2.)

25 They were those of Reuben Arap Seroney to Leah (Jeptorus), Mika Arap Bomet to Marta (Jebui) and Andrew Arap Kimaiyo to Jemilo, and are the earliest for which I can trace any record.

26 The Nandi called them *barasa* from the Swahili *baraza* meaning a 'public assembly'.

27 G.W.B. **Huntingford,** *The Southern Nilo-Hamites,* pp. 36-7.

28 African Courts Ordinance No. 65 of 1951.

29 Cf. Arthur Phillips, 'Divorce by Judicial Process' in Arthur Phillips and Henry F. Morris, *Marriage Laws in Africa,* London, 1971 (1953), p. 121 and my 'Ritual Change among the Nandi', n. 25, p. 274.

30 Republic of Kenya, *Report of the Commission on the Law of Marriage and Divorce,* Nairobi, 1968. The Report proposes to make all marriages subject to laws of compulsory registration.

31 In Nandi *kiilgei,* literally 'to anoint each other'. The same verb, *il,* also means 'to break'; I suggest, therefore, a play on the word's double meaning. Perhaps the custom of 'anointing' goes back to a common heritage with the Kipsigis rather than being a recent innovation of the Nandi.

32 G.W.B. Huntingford, in mentioning the custom of 'anointing' at divorce, confuses the issue by referring to it as symbolising 'separation' at one point and 'reconciliation' at another, and not explaining why (*Nandi Work and Culture*, p. 10).

33 All names are fictitious; otherwise the facts are as I found them in the records at Kapsabet.

34 Case No. cc 15/60 and cc 253/60 in the Appeal Court, Kapsabet, and African Court, Kabiyet, respectively.

35 Case No. cc 11/59 and cc 100/59 at the Appeal Court, Kapsabet.

36 The implication of this is that either the man's first wife was betrothed to him long before she was due to be circumcised or that he married his second wife while the first was in seclusion.

37 Case heard at Chemundu on 17 April 1957.

38 Case heard at Chemundu on 26 April and 9 September 1958.

39 Case at Chemundu dated 26 April and 9 September 1958.

40 Case at Chemundu dated 20 October and 30 November 1959.

41 Cases heard at Kabiyet on 24 April 1973 and 17 April 1973.

42 Case heard at Kapsabet, dated 15 September 1972 and 29 January 1973.

43 Civil Case No. 44 of 1972 at Kapsabet.

44 Civil Case No. 5/1/1971 at Kapsabet.

45 See notes 1, 3 above.

46 Arap Rogok and Alexander Rotich at Kaptumo on 27 November 1973 and others.

VIII. The Ritual Symbolism

Nandi ritual is rich in symbols. The exegesis which follows is offered on the basis of a detailed knowledge of Nandi ritual and against the background of various interpreters' attempts to explain symbolic systems.[1]

1. Symbols of Passage

It has been said in retrospect that in distinguishing three phases in a *rite de passage* Arnold van Gennep was merely stating the obvious: every life crisis ritual has a beginning, a middle and an end.[2] Be that as it may; when applied to Nandi ritual his schema — separation, transition and incorporation — helps considerably in distinguishing not only a general symbolic pattern but useful categories in which to place individual symbols.

(i) Separation

In all four rituals described above significant emphasis is laid on announcing the event to the community in advance. Take, for example, the female initiation ritual. Members of kindred group, clan and neighbourhood are notified of the impending ceremony. And as the initiand travels about the community announcing the date of her initiation she is marked out as separated from women and children alike. The symbols of separation which she possesses are fly whisk, bells and whistle.

The main symbols of separation, however, appear to be those which distinguish the candidate (male or female) from the rest of the community and at the same time identify him/her with his/her fellow candidates or, at least, a new group. Such are shaving of the hair, anointing with oil, transvestism, mutilation of the sex organ, song-and-dance, degrees of uncleanness, the ritual cutting and collecting of firewood, and rending of the bag.[3]

(ii) Transition

It is during the initiation rites that liminality is most strongly emphasised. The anomalous position of a liminal personage is marked by symbols of liminality such as nakedness, painting of the body, transvestism and lack of status.[4] It is, however, worth noting that even during their period of seclusion at the initiation lodge Nandi youths, traditionally, were ordered in accordance with the norms of social structure. After their wedding ceremony the newly-wed couple enter the transitional stage of being catered for by the bridegroom's mother; they may even reside in her house for several days.

(iii) *Incorporation*

The re-aggregation of candidates into society is emphasised in all four rites. In initiation it is marked by symbols such as immersion, frightening and testing, taking the oath, unveiling and homecoming. In marriage it is begun by the tying of the ritual grass with accompanying ritual and completed by the handing over of the bridewealth when the two kindred groups are united by mutual exchange of wealth. In divorce it is achieved when the former husband and wife turn their backs on one another and return to their respective communities as marriageable adults.

2. *Pastoral Symbols*

One cannot read Audrey Richards' *Chisungu* without being struck by certain contrasts between Bemba and Nandi symbolism. This is particularly obvious in the Bemba use of symbols related to cultivation and the Nandi employment of what I term 'pastoral symbolism'.[5] All that is meant by 'pastoral symbolism' is a symbolism apparently originating in the natural environment of a pastoral people.

Probably the most frequently occurring of these pastoral symbols is milk. Mixed with water or beer or pure and unadulterated it is expectorated in blessing. Churned and clarified it is used to anoint in cementing relationship ties. Curdled in gourds it is not only a staple food but the ritual drink of initiands and warriors at initiation, actors at a wedding and other significant participants in a ritual. Milk is important in itself: it is essential for the survival of a pastoral people and its abundance means health and fertility for man and beast. But like all symbols, it has a reference beyond itself to ideas and actions of great consequence for society.

Associated with milk is its container, the gourd or calabash, used ritually on several occasions. During the male initiation ritual a cowrie-decorated warrior's gourd placed on top of the table-like arch symbolises male virility and at the same time acts as a vehicle of instruction for the initiand. During the marriage ritual a gourd is employed to represent a baby, and its milk contents are drunk by the young attendant of the bride. Here both the physical shape of the gourd and its function as a milk container are significant. I was explicitly informed that in the latter instance it is the 'sign of children'.[6]

Another dominant symbol directly related to the cattle economy is cowdung. Mixed with shaven hair it is smeared around the base of the shrine during initiation and again at marriage. It is similarly employed at the base of an arch erected during the seclusion of male initiands. Associated with it in the latter-mentioned instance is cow's urine stepped into by the initiands and poured on their bare bodies 'as a blessing to show appreciation for cattle'. Undoubtedly, because of its connection with cattle it already possesses ritual value, but this is enhanced by a 'mystical' significance acquired through its use at the shrine.[7]

Cattle symbolism, and to a lesser extent that of sheep and goats, is of course largely ubiquitous in Nandi ritual. Ox-hide, goatskin and sheepskin have become ritual clothing. This means that nowadays when animal skins are brought out only for ritual and ceremonial occasions their symbolic significance is enhanced. 'Ritual happenings' such as betrothal and marriage take place not in the living room of a Nandi house but in the animal quarters. Traditional dancing evokes the image of cattle passing through the gate into the enclosure. More explicitly, the initiands crawl like cattle through the table-like arch constructed in the house of *tumdo* while at the same time they are whistled to like cattle coming from the river. The structure is variously termed, two of the most common names being 'cow' or 'cow's stomach'. The container filled with clarified butter for anointing is a specially-decorated ox-horn used on ritual occasions, while grass, the fodder of cattle, is treated with reverence by Nandi generally. The animals themselves, together with sheep and goats, are used for purposes of divination and sacrifice, and of course for the all-important substance of bridewealth. Finally, throughout the male initiation ritual implements connected with cattle are given prominence for decorative and didactic purposes.

To conclude this section I wish to make two points. First, it has been suggested by Victor Turner that initiation rites often draw their symbolism from the situation of parturition and first lactation, where in nature blood, water, faeces and milk are present.[8] I am not going to deny the likelihood that Nandi initiation rites draw their symbolism from the situation of parturition and first lactation, but rather suggest that they draw it from their pastoral situation also. It is not a question of either/or, but of both/and. Second, I should like to suggest that the Nandi use of pastoral symbolism at times approaches the position where the symbol is imbued with 'magical' or at least 'efficacious' powers to make real the thing symbolised. Take, for example, the ritual enactment of the hoped-for role of parenthood by bride and groom and their young attendants at a wedding ceremony. In this instance the connection between symbolic enactment and actual event appears to be a causal one: the dramatisation of parental roles, or so I was informed, ensures a fruitful union.[9]

3. Structural Symbols

By structural symbols I mean those symbols which both reflect and are intended to help reinforce the structures of society.

When initiands take their place in the ritual procession according to the age-set seniority of their fathers, or share in the ritual cutting of firewood with fellow initiands their acts take on symbolic significance reflecting and reinforcing Nandi social structures. However, not only the initiands themselves but all participants in the ritual take their place according to similar rules of priority. The age-set and age-grade institution is so strongly reinforced that it overrides the cancelling out of status distinctions during the period of transition.

When preparations are being made for initiation or negotiations are under way concerning marriage, members and elders of kindred group, clan and neighbourhood are notified. In the past, of course, in addition, the sanction of the chief ritual expert — the *Laibon* — had to be obtained for initiation. Moreover, members of the important social groupings played their part in the ritual proceedings and took their respective places around the ritual beer-pot.

Right indicates male, left female, and so men sit on the right and women on the left, for example at the betrothal ceremony. The grass is tied on the right wrist of the male and on the left wrist of the female. During the male initiation ritual implements used by men are placed to the right on the table-like arch, while those used by women are placed to the left. Not only is this an indication of sex differences but also of the dominance of the male, as is the long decorated gourd of the warrior and the transvestiture of the female initiand in warrior's dress. So too the division of labour is clearly marked throughout the ritual sequence: women cooking, men eating, the bride looking after the children and the groom herding the flocks.

Initiation means inclusion in Nandi society; failure to be initiated means exclusion. The rituals symbolically reinforce this. Uninitiated males (except of course the initiands themselves) may not take part in the initiation ceremonies. Uncircumcised females are not allowed into the inner circle during the anointing at the shrine, or during the operation itself. Similarly, neither unmarried males nor unmarried females may take part in the marriage ritual.

To sum up, the political ordering of the age-set and age-grade systems, the social ordering of kindred group, clan and neighbourhood, the sexual ordering of male and female roles and the tribal ordering of the uninitiated and the initiated all combine to give rise to a symbolism which in turn reinforces the structures.

I have not emphasised significantly the patrilineal nature of Nandi social structures, but its importance may be observed in the roles played by the mother's brother and the paternal kin. Indeed, a contrast might be made here also between the symbolism of the patrilineal Nandi and that of the matrilineal Bemba described by Richards.

4. *Religious Symbols*

To those who observe or participate in Nandi ritual today, religious symbols are by far the most elusive and obscure. It took time before I became aware of their existence, not to speak of their pervasiveness and significance. It was only after the repeated insistence of Christian informants that they could not take part in the traditional rites, or at least certain parts of them, because of their religious significance, that I eventually forsook my previously-held view that such insistence was missionary-inspired, and proceeded to piece together what information I could glean from literature, oral tradition and current practice.[10]

At an exegetical level I received little help as most informants possessed scant knowledge as to interpretation. It was to questions concerning the origin or significance of religious symbols that people most often replied: 'We do so-and-so because *Mong'o* said so.'[11] Most of my conclusions in this area are therefore tentative and based on the interpretation of the symbols at operational and positional levels.[12]

On the surface, life crisis rituals in Nandi appear to be 'non-religious' or 'secular'. But this initial impression is not borne out by the facts. The fact of the matter is that religious symbols and appeals to *Asis* in prayer occur frequently throughout these and other Nandi rituals.

For example, let us take first of all the shrine or bunch of ritual plants placed outside the back door of a Nandi house. Much of the significance underlying and surrounding the shrine has been lost. What is certain is that in its use today, at initiation and marriage rituals, it is a highly-condensed religious symbol related to the worship of *Asis*.[13]

Secondly, let us take two things associated with the shrine (or in the past, the place of sacrifice): animals which were slaughtered and plants which were burnt. When animals are slaughtered today and ritual plants burnt, the animals (by the appearance of their entrails) and the plants (by the manner of the ascending smoke) tell out the auspicious or inauspicious nature of the omens.[14] Also associated with the shrine, although not solely so, is the rite of 'anointing with oil'.[15] Interestingly enough, it has been suggested that the Kipsigis word for a similar kind of structure to the Nandi shrine is derived from a combination of *ma*, meaning 'place' and *mwaita*, meaning 'oil'. If this is so, the anointing takes on mystical significance because of its connection with the place of sacrifice and prayer to *Asis* and confirms the connotation of 'blessing' indicated by some of my informants.

Thirdly, let us examine the use of the number 'four', also associated with the shrine but with wider references as well, and from there proceed to look at the ritual employment of other numbers and some Nandi decorative motifs. Four times the shrine is encircled, four times clarified butter is applied, four times immersion is undergone, four times the elders expectorate the mixture of milk and beer in blessing, and so we could go on. But nobody could give the reason, beyond affirming that *Mong'o* said so. Aidan Southall, in a recent essay, follows J.G. Peristiany (although quoting a Kipsigis, Richard Koech) in interpreting 'four' to mean 'male' and 'three' 'female' among the Kipsigis.[16] Nowhere, however, have I been able to confirm this suggestion for the Nandi: that whereas males perform an action four times, females perform the same action thrice. Rather, the use of the circle in decorative motifs variously depicted with emphasised central point, radiating ribs, or intersecting cross, suggests sun-symbolism and possibly a symbolism that is universal.[17] So too does the association of the number 'nine' with *Asis*: one of *Asis*'s appellations meaning 'daughter of the nine legs (or rays) of the sun' is interpreted by the Nandi to mean 'the omnipotent one', by the Kipsigis to mean 'the infinite' and conjures up the image of the wheel or *mandala*, well-known universal symbols.[18] Furthermore, I was repeatedly given both the numbers 'four' and 'eight' as the correct number of ritual plants to employ in the construction of the shrine. Also of significance is that 'eight' was most likely the original number of the Nandi age-set cycle and 'four' the number of sub-sets in each set.[19] In universal symbolism 'four' is often referred to the four cardinal points.

The religious symbolism of Nandi, therefore, is highly suggestive of the forms of symbolism employed by *homo religiosus* throughout the ages: sun-symbolism, quadripartite symbolism and the symbolically significant circle, wheel or *mandala*.[20] Moreover, the latter appears eminently suitable to depict the Nandi idea of the ultimate orderliness and wholeness of life embodied in their cosmology. In sum, Nandi religious symbolism suggests the 'degree of symbolic elaboration and coherence' which one writer regrets has been lacking in the ethnographic studies of East African peoples.[21]

A further point of contrast might be made between the religious symbolism of the Bemba and the Nandi. The Nandi appear to be pre-occupied with worship of *Asis* and the related sun-symbolism, the Bemba expend much energy placating the ancestors.[22]

5. Symbols Interpreted

(i) Shaving the Head

Discussing the subject of hair as a public symbol Raymond Firth writes:

> But on the whole, deliberate shaving of the head, or close cutting of the hair, has taken on a ritual quality, intended to mark a transition from one social state to another, and in particular to imply a modification in the status or social condition of the person whose hair is so treated ... [23]

There is every indication that shaving of the head in Nandi has precisely this meaning. My informants said that both boys and girls were normally called 'liminal personages' after the ritual act of shaving the head. Admittedly, particularly nowadays, in the girl's rite this distinction is left until after the physical operation itself. But the similarity between 'cutting the hair' and 'cutting the sex organs' is obvious. To confirm the interpretation: bride and groom have the head shaven after the tying of the grass; if it is the man's first marriage he has his head completely shaven, if his second or more then the hair is only partially removed above the ears. And significantly, the bride-wealth is not transferred until the groom's family has been sent word that the couple's new hair has begun to grow — a period of about two weeks.

(ii) *Anointing*

'The reason for anointing is to make her fear nothing' states an informant about a girl being prepared to undergo clitoridectomy; its purpose is 'to show that the girl is going to be theirs at marriage' writes another. In mentioning Kipsigis anointing Peristiany writes generally of 'blessing',[24] while ethnographers of other East African peoples fail to offer any explanation. I have only one suggestion, which may hold good for the Nandi but possibly not for the Kipsigis. There is an apparent contradiction in Nandi between the anointing at initiation and marriage, which obviously 'unites' in the cementing of relationships, and the anointing at one form of the divorce ritual which 'separates'. Or is there? I am inclined to think not. At initiation and marriage it is those between whom sexual intercourse is forbidden who anoint each other and at the divorce it is man and wife, a couple who vow never to resume sexual relations, who anoint one another.

(iii) *Cutting of Wood*

The ritual wielding of the axe and cutting of firewood is expressly stated by Nandi to indicate togetherness and unity. There is no doubt that ritually it symbolises that solidarity felt by those men who sat around the same circumcision fire, thus belonging to the same sub-set and age-set in the age-grade organisation and the women who shared the same festivities and instruction before clitoridectomy — a brief experience of what Victor Turner terms *communitas*.[25] The action also helps to reinforce the social order and reassert the world-view. This is due to the performance of the act according to strict ritual order and the use of the symbolic number 'four'.

(iv) *Obscenity, Antagonism and Rebellion*

There is nothing to indicate that the use of obscenity, antagonism and rebellion generally, in Nandi, either within or without the ritual sequence, is any different from that reported from other societies. The literature provides us with numerous examples of ceremonies in which people from the lower echelons of society are made temporary rulers and in which women act out male roles and vice versa. Undoubtedly, as Max Gluckman suggests, these rites of reversal include 'a protest against the established order' while at the same time they are 'intended to preserve and even to strengthen' that same order.[26] Indeed, in many rituals their performance is believed to achieve success and prosperity for the group which practises them. Such licence of role reversal is to be found in Nandi ritual when warriors at the beginning of a new-age-set cycle break all norms of sexual behaviour, when during initiation male initiands don female clothing and female initiands put on warriors' ceremonial dress, and when during ritual song-and-dance sequences obscene, ribald or coarse language is indulged in.

It is my belief, however, that the theory of 'protest' does not exhaust the meaning: the simple theory of 'catharsis' may also be relevant. Catharsis is felt when tensions existing between the sexes, clans and kindred groups are brought into the open by means of ribaldry. Normally, Nandi social conversation is very proper and circumspect; normally, women respect men; and in sexual relations the male dominates. But not so when initiands are being given encouragement or during the singing of circumcision and marriage songs generally. There, the use of language is akin to the stories of British pantomime and the jokes of the concert hall or BBC entertainer; and they have a similar cathartic effect.

A particularly good example of an action to be placed in the category of inversion or rebellion is the resistance of the bride to her husband's first sexual advances.[27] From henceforth the woman will submit and she must be taught by experience. One of the most important lessons to be learnt by a new bride is that she must never — no matter how busily occupied — refuse the sexual advances of her husband.

(v) *Transvestiture*

Transvestism occurs in both male and female initiation rites. In the past, these occurrences were parallel, whereas today it is difficult to recognise any correlation. Traditionally, at the same time in both rites, soon after the shaving of the head at the beginning of the phase of separation, male initiands had their clothes taken by their friends whereupon they were dressed in girls' attire and girl candidates were clad in warriors' dress by their 'sweethearts'. Likewise, after the operation, male initiands were clad in women's skirts for the first few days of their convalescence in seclusion. Girls, however, during their seclusion were also clad in women's skirts. Nowadays men are no longer clothed in women's garments, rather they are bedecked with headsquares and jewellery during the opening dance. The transvestiture of the girl, however, is another matter: it has assumed increasing importance. Indeed, to the observer it appears to be the focal point of social attention and the ritual high point of the modern female initiation rite.

In Nandi, the positional level of interpretation points to 'liminality' and 'confusion' because transvestism in both male and female rites occurs after the shaving of the hair during the period of transition from an uninitiated to an initiated state.[28] The new identity of being an adult Nandi has not yet been forged: the boy is not yet a man, the girl is not yet a woman but neither are they still children — their status is an ambivalent one.

The field context and social structure of the Nandi point to other possible interpretations of the transvestiture of the young female initiand in warrior's dress, particularly as practised at present.

First, it points to inversion or role reversal, as discussed above. Normally a Nandi woman is mindful of the respect she owes her husband and of the submissive role she must play in relation to men generally. Now she acts the part of an aggressive warrior in splendid ceremonial dress while literally everybody and everything revolve around her. By reversing her role and inverting the order she strengthens the established structures and maintains the cosmological balance. In addition, her femininity, her ability to beget children, is affirmed, indeed positively assured.

Secondly, it points to rebellion. Some women unconsciously resent their lot and here through transvestism they briefly assume the dominant role.

Thirdly, and not unrelated to the former, the transvestiture of the female initiand in elaborate warriors' dress appears to reflect the high value placed on warriorhood. Interestingly enough it is only the transvestism belonging to the female rite which has survived to any extent in Nandi ritual to the present day. Its persistence must be for some significant reason, a reason to be found by exploring the way in which the symbol has been allowed to develop.

The reader will recall that the warriors' dress worn by the girl before clitoridectomy is an expensive, highly elaborate version of what the Nandi warrior used to wear. It resembles very closely the ceremonial dress worn at public celebrations today. It represents the splendour of the Nandi warrior in bygone days, but includes many more elements in addition. My suggestion is that it has become a highly-condensed symbol of what it means to be a Nandi — of 'Nandiness' — as has the rite of clitoridectomy in general. The colobus monkey skin leglets and epaulettes and the jangling thigh-bells recall the Nandi warrior in his heyday: terror of the surrounding peoples, victor over the war-happy

Maasai, menace of the Uganda Railway and thorn-in-the-flesh to the colonial administration. The headdress in national colours, bedecked with medals from both World Wars and the orange 'kilt' of jinja cotton, resemble the modern warrior's dress worn at traditional dances and on public occasions, and represent the Nandi acceptance of inevitable change. The intricate beadwork on leather belts, the embroidery and stitching on the headdress underline the woman's continued domestic role but the 'butterfly' sleeves of numerous headsquares point to the new status of women in society. So also the 'non-iron' shirt and the school tie represent the modern Nandi youth influenced by the change instigated by trader, administrator, missionary and teacher. But that is not all. The modern Nandi youth has a part to play in the affairs of the nation and so he sports a badge bearing the image of President Kenyatta. So too he has a part to play in the world of international sport and this is symbolised by the track boots which call to mind the running feats of Kipchoge Keino and Ben Jipcho. Significantly, some of the same themes run through the initiation songs.

In sum, transvestism has developed beyond all recognition, making the occasion of clitoridectomy, both for the initiand and the neighbourhood, an affirmation of what it means to be a Nandi in the 1970s.

(vi) *Colour*

Colour symbolism plays a minor role in Nandi ritual. But the triad of colours, red, white and black, does occur.

Red is the colour of blood and life. It is the colour applied to warriors in particular, although, in the past, women also employed it to a lesser extent. Obviously used for cosmetic purposes it also had practical benefits: the fat with which it was applied provided insulation against heat and cold; and the ochre itself, when applied with water, removed the fat and body dirt through absorption.

White is written of by psychologists as possessing 'sacred' and 'god-like' connotations. Although the Nandi refer to *Asis* as the 'white' or 'shining' one, there is no evidence to suggest that the classification of white in Nandi ritual refers to divinity. White, of course, is the colour of milk and of semen. The ritual climbing plant, employed extensively in the initiation ritual, is stated to have milky sap. Referring to the Maasai, Andrew Fedders says that when not actually used milk is symbolised by a mixture of white chalk and water; this mixture is applied in Nandi to the male initiand who has lost an elder sibling through death, and to any male initiand while in seclusion.[29] If white is related to milk and puberty and therefore to femininity these two instances would exemplify inverse symbolism similar to that exemplified by transvestism. If, on the other hand, white is related to semen then these instances would exemplify the usage of a simple fertility symbol. Possibly, too, 'whiteness' approaches having a magical effect, or it may simply indicate transition and confusion.[30]

Black has been interpreted by Victor Turner in one instance as originating from its association with alluvial soil and symbolising 'fertility and marital love'.[31] I have no suggestion to make as to what black symbolises in Nandi. For example, it is required that the hide on which a newly-married couple sleep should be black and white, yet no interpretation is offered.

As for the origin of the triad, red, white and black: cattle, sheep and goats are red, white or black or a mixture of all three. Red is the colour of blood, soil and ochre; white is the colour of milk, semen and chalk; black is the colour of charcoal and alluvial soil.

(vii) *Ordeals*

Ordeals are a feature of the initiation rites of all the Kalenjin and many other East and Central African peoples. As for their meaning, the Nandi repeatedly assert that their purpose is to inculcate courage or bravery — a major theme in Nandi culture. I have found no reason to disagree with this stated aim, rather the reverse: because nowadays young people often justify the continuing practice of circumcision by appealing to its success in making a confident and mature adult out of a child. It is precisely this kind of success which leads Audrey Richards to credit the ordeals with a magical quality.[32] I would stop short of this, but at the same time would underline that ordeals are not simply endurance tests but techniques to help impart skills and inculcate courage: skills of weapon making, hunting and raiding in the case of men and of domestic affairs in the case of women; courage to endure the cold highland nights and the extremely cold waters of rivers in flood. Moreover, the degree of emphasis on failure in meeting the requirements of elders and warriors is sensible and balanced. Those who are not quite up to standard are given further training and subjected to a second test. And when some measure of flinching at pain is to be expected, the singing and cheering of the crowd increase.

(viii) *The Arch*

The emphasis on bravery and passage from childhood to adult state appears to be greater in the male than in the female rite. This is to be expected. It is borne out by the more frequent occurrence of the arch in the boys' ritual as over against the girls' — according to my informants, three times in the former and once in the latter. The occasion common to both is the construction of the arch in the river dam at immersion. Nandi exegesis compares the arch to a 'cow', 'cow's legs', a 'cow's stomach' or the 'vagina of an elephant'. Certainly the implication is one of traumatic and painful birth. If ordeals have any effectual powers then the excruciating pain endured on some of these occasions must ensure that the Nandi youth becomes an adult. From the 'womb' of the arch a Nandi is born.[33]

(ix) *Seclusion*

Related to the foregoing is the symbolic significance of seclusion. Presumably, seclusion signifies 'death'. Through dying one re-enters the 'womb' to be eventually reborn in the waters of immersion.

(x) *Immersion*

One simply needs to mention here the cleansing and new birth either implied or explicitly referred to above and to re-emphasise the practical significance of the event as an endurance test and final means of inculcating courage.

(xi) *Enactment*

The role enactment at marriage of the bride and groom as parents and their attendants as nursemaid and herdsboy has been mentioned before. It is sufficient to draw attention here to the 'magical' or 'efficacious' nature of the symbolic act. By explicit interpretation of the Nandi themselves, this act comes nearer than any other to creating the situation dramatised.

(xii) *Binding*

The tying of the grass at betrothal and marriage and the tying of the leather thong before emerging from the seclusion of initiation denote the binding nature of the acts. So the Nandi explicitly interpret them, adding the suggestion that the painful jerking of the thong round the little finger acts as an aid to memory.

(xiii) *Rending the Bag*

Both context and cosmology offer help in interpreting this unusual symbol — unusual in the sense of the soil being allowed to spill to the ground. The words spoken on oath include the phrase 'this soil eat me' and the Nandi world-view envisages a dead man's 'soul' entering into the underworld as the hyena goes to earth. This would suggest that the soil signifies 'death': until death the couple never shall unite, or so they vow. It is conceivable that the soil falling may ensure the break: it may be yet one more example of symbolic enactment.

6. Ideas Symbolised

In conclusion I should like to enumerate the main ideas symbolised in Nandi ritual. The exercise will serve as a convenient method of recapitulation.

Death and rebirth are symbolised in the very notion of *rites de passage* and specifically in the ordeals of seclusion and passing through the arch erected in the river dam. Order is constantly upheld through the playing of appropriate roles and the reinforcement of the social structure in word, action and song. Conflict, particularly between the sexes, is played out during the songs and dances and through the transvestiture of the female in warrior's dress. Fertility is a pervasive theme, and besides its use of pastoral imagery employs the medium of ritual plants such as the milky creeper, *sinendet*, and the knotty *nogirwet* stick. Cosmology, affirming the right relationship of a Nandi to *Asis* and the environment of nature, man and beast, is reflected throughout the rites, for example in the encircling of the shrine and turning towards the east.

NOTES

1 On 'symbols' and 'symbolism' see: C.G. Jung, *Man and His Symbols*, London, 1964, pp. 20-21, 93; Edward Sapir, 'Symbolism' from *Encyclopaedia of the Social Sciences*, Vol. XIV, New York, 1934, pp. 492-5 and reprinted in *Writings of Edward Sapir*; Victor W. Turner, 'Symbols in African Ritual' in Janet L. Dolgin, David S. Kemnitzer, and David M. Schneider (eds), *Symbolic Anthropology: A Reader in the Study of Symbols and Meanings*, New York, 1977, pp. 183-94, also his 'Symbols in Ndembu Ritual' in *The Forest of Symbols*, Ithaca, New York, 1967, pp. 19-47, and 'Three Symbols of *Passage* in Ndembu Circumcision Ritual: *An Interpretation*' in Max Gluckman (ed.), *Essays on the Ritual of Social Relations*, Manchester, 1962, pp. 124-73; Max Gluckman, *Politics, Law and Ritual in Tribal Society*, Oxford, 1965, p. 252; Monica Wilson, 'Nyakyusa Ritual and Symbolism' in *American Anthropologist*, Vol. LVI, No. 2, Part I, April 1954, pp. 228-41; Eugene L. Hartley, 'Symbolism' in *A Dictionary of the Social Sciences*, London, 1964, pp. 711-12; Mary Douglas, *Natural Symbols*, Harmondsworth, 1973, passim; Aylward Shorter, *African Culture and the Christian Church*, London, 1973, pp. 89-92; Dan Sperber, *Rethinking Symbolism*, Cambridge, 1975; Philip L. Ravenhill, 'The Interpretation of Symbolism in Wan Female Initiation' in *Africa*, Vol. XLVIII, No. 1, 1978, pp. 66-79; Marja-Liisa Swantz, *Ritual and Symbol in Transitional Zaramo Society*, Lund, 1970, passim.

2 Arnold van Gennep, *The Rites of Passage*, Chicago/London, 1960. (First published as *Les rites de passage*, 1908, and translated from the French by Monika B. Vizedom and Gabrielle L. Caffee.)

3 Transvestism has characteristics of both separation and transition because of the paradoxical nature of a female in male dress.

4   See Victor W. Turner, *The Ritual Process,* pp. 95-6, on the marks of liminality.

5   Audrey I. Richards, *Chisungu: A Girls' Initiation Ceremony among the Bemba of Northern Rhodesia,* London, 1956, esp. pp. 70-76.

6   Kapsabet schoolgirl, June 1973.

7   See G.W.B. Huntingford, *The Southern Nilo-Hamites,* p. 20.

8   Victor W. Turner, 'Colour Classification in Ndembu Ritual', in M. Banton (ed.), *Anthropological Approaches to the Study of Religion,* London, 1966, p. 173.

9   Cf. Mary Douglas on the Eucharist, *Natural Symbols,* pp. 69-72 and Monica Wilson 'Nyakyusa Ritual and Symbolism', loc. cit., pp. 235-7.

10 I have appended the bulk of these findings to my thesis 'Ritual Change among the Nandi' in a study entitled '*Koros*', pp. 342-54.

11 *Mong'o* or *Bamong'o*, the mythical ancestor of the Nandi, is believed to have laid down the rules of Nandi ritual procedure.

12 Victor Turner speaks of symbols as *multivocal* or *polysemous,* meaning that they stand for many things at once, each having a 'fan' or 'spectrum' of referents. As such, symbols have three 'levels' or 'fields' of meaning. The first level, which he terms *exegetical,* represents the interpretation of those who use the symbols; the second level, of *operational* meaning, is obtained from observing how the symbol is used in the immediate context; the third level, of *positional* meaning, is found in examining a symbol's relationship to its more remote context, to the other situations in which the image is used.

13 See the Appendix, '*Koros*', cited above.

14 G.W.B. Huntingford, *The Southern Nilo-Hamites,* p. 52.

15 The 'oil' is clarified butter.

16 Aidan Southall, 'Twinship and Symbolic Structure' in J.S. La Fontaine (ed.), *The Interpretation of Ritual,* London, 1972, p. 90. See also J.G. Peristiany, *The Social Institutions of the Kipsigis,* p. 10.

17 The motifs are as follows: ⊙ ⊕ ⊕ ⊕

18 Cf. Émile Durkheim, *The Elementary Forms of the Religious Life,* London, 1915, pp. 379-83, 127, also Aniela Jaffé, 'Symbolism in the Visual Arts' in C.G. Jung, op. cit., p. 240.

19 See my 'Ritual Change among the Nandi', pp. 36-7.

20 C.G. Jung, op. cit., pp. 20, 21-2, 42.

21 Aidan Southall, loc. cit., pp. 92-3.

22 Richards, op. cit., pp. 63, 88-9, 90, 119, 139, 142-5, 146, 167, 183-4, 200; cf. Christopher Ehret, 'Some Possible Trends in Precolonial Religious Thought in Kenya and Tanzania', paper read at the Conference on the Historical Study of African Religions, Nairobi, June 1974, p. 5.

23 Raymond Firth, *Symbols: Public and Private,* London, 1974, p. 289.

24 Peristiany, op. cit., p. 64.

25 Turner, *The Ritual Process,* pp. 94-130.

26 See my 'Ritual Change among the Nandi', pp. 114-18; also Max Gluckman, *Custom and Conflict in Africa,* Oxford, 1956, p. 109.

27 Cf. Max Gluckman, *Rituals of Rebellion in South-East Africa,* Manchester, 1954, pp. 5-24; E.E. Evans-Pritchard, 'Some Collective Expressions of Obscenity in Africa' in his *The Position of Women in Primitive Societies and Other Essays in Social Anthropology,* London, 1965, p. 101.

28 Cf. Turner, loc. cit., and also his 'Symbols in Ndembu Ritual', loc. cit., p. 42.
29 Cynthia Salvadori and Andrew Fedders, *Maasai*, London, 1973, p. 23.
30 On the symbolism of 'semen' among the Dorze of Ethiopia see Dan Sperber, *Rethinking Symbolism*, pp. 37-42.
31 Turner, 'Colour Classification in Ndembu Ritual', loc. cit., p. 173.
32 Richards, op. cit., p. 123.
33 Richards, op. cit., p. 64 and Turner, *The Ritual Process*, p. 67.

IX. The Ritual Change

Can ritual exist in a rapidly changing society? I am certain that it can and must because what it expresses is, at the deepest level, constant; it is the acceptance of birth and death, of growth and change, of the dependence of man on God ...

Monica Wilson[1]

1. *Perspectives on Change*

The *traditionalist*, looking back to the turn of the century, regrets the passing of much that he considers authentically Nandi: the respect of the young for the old, of women for men; the proud bearing of a brave warrior tribe; the training in behaviour and skills; the ritual restrictions on the drinking of beer; the strict moral discipline of the young; the code of sexual behaviour and much else besides. In accounting for the passing of these virtues and the prevalence of current social ills he will first of all recall the coming of Arab trading caravans and the Uganda Railway. The latter in particular brought about the spoliation of Nandi womenfolk by coolies and soldiers and led to their turning to prostitution and its attendant evil — economic and social independence! He will then lament the killing of the Nandi *Laibon*, Koitalel Arap Samoei, the imposition of British rule, the settling of Nandi land, the 'rising' of 1923 and the subsequent outlawing of the ceremony to mark the handing over of authority to a new generation of warriors. These acts of aggression spelt the end of the Nandi warrior and his way of life and imposed a foreign-dominated hierarchy of chiefs in place of the elders chosen traditionally by natural selection to rule the people. The authority of the elders was challenged and gradually eroded. Next he will turn to the political, economic and social advantages which accrued to those who betrayed the tribe and collaborated with government and mission alike. They and their children failed to honour *Asis* and refused to undergo the rites of circumcision. Then with great savour he will recount how the children of the first Nandi Christian woman to remain uncircumcised were either dead or deformed. The total picture is one of unrelieved gloom.[2]

The *Christian* considers the origins and effects of change from a different perspective. True, like the traditionalist, he laments the passing of a moral order with something of the same sense of dismay, but it is a different kind of order and, moreover, he sees the change over a shorter time-span and from within what we might call a Christian 'sub-culture'. Elders of the church take second wives. Why? Daughters of Christian parents become pregnant before marriage. Why? Boys and girls go through traditional circumcision rites unlike

126

their parents. Why? Christian men join together to form co-operatives, buy land in the settlement areas to the north of Nandi, then in most cases fail to attend church again. Why? Discipline is failing in schools; boys circumcised too young think they are men and disobey their uncircumcised teachers. Why? Christian men and women attend beer-drinks and circumcision parties. Why? In most cases blame is attached to youth but in other instances there is genuine perplexity both as to the origins and effects of change. However, I ought not to omit mentioning the other type of Nandi Christian leader who turns a blind eye to many facts and pretends that all is well.[3]

The *young person*, Christian or otherwise, suffers most acutely from lack of identity. On the whole, he does not know who he is or where he is going. He certainly has opinions but although expressed with passion and articulated with vigour they seldom spring from an integrated personality or a coherent system of values. 'Circumcision is mutilation of the bodily organs which were created for a purpose; the Bible says so.' 'Circumcision is all right for boys but not for girls.' 'For biological reasons a girl ought not to be circumcised, a boy must.' 'Circumcision is necessary to uphold the traditions of Nandi.' 'I am worried about the next generation: they won't know to which age-set they belong and all people will have the same rights.' Missionaries, teachers and politicians vie with each other for the allegiance of Nandi youth. Confusion reigns.[4]

To the *observer* or *social anthropologist* much of the change appears inevitable and he can view it with a certain amount of detachment. He will see what the traditionalist can never see: remarkable stability in the face of economic, social and political upheaval. He will see differences between Catholic and Protestant attitudes to culture, noting how the Africa Inland Church in particular appeared to substitute a form of Christian legalism for the traditional code of morals: in translation to another culture gospel very soon became law. He will note the effects of this on Christian disaffection and also the fact that the first Nandi converts were influenced while away from the tribal scene, in the city, on the farm, or in the army barrack

2. *A Highly-Classified Society*

Why this stability which the social anthropologist is able to detect? The first and obvious answer lies in the Nandi social system. Traditionally it was characterised by high classification. It had a highly-developed system of shared classifications in which individuals were strongly controlled by other people's (group) pressure.[5] So much so that although there is evidence to suggest that colonialism upset Nandi equilibrium to an extent — particularly in the years preceding and following the Second World War when the role of the sexes and the division of labour were affected by the exodus of Nandi

womenfolk to fight under the British flag — it did not upset it too
unduly. For the Nandi, as compared with their Bantu and Nilotic
neighbours, maintained a measure of stability and a certain degree of
resistance to change.[6] Even today theirs is not the way of founding
numerous sects and independent churches, forming themselves into
politically-motivated tribal societies or spawning gangs of rebellious
and dissident youths as is the case with the surrounding Luyia and
Luo.

However, I wish to explore the subject from another angle. From
the rites described above I have selected a number of dominant ritual
symbols, the majority of them highly-condensed, all of them conventional. And by distinguishing between 'logico-meaningful' and
'causal-functional' integration in society, I want to suggest why in a
period of rapid change in Nandi some of these symbols have *persisted*,
some have *developed* and yet others have become *extinct*.[7] By this
means I hope to show that there exists a certain amount of correlation
between a society's handling of ritual in a period of change and its
maintenance of stability and social order.

The symbols selected are six in number and are as follows: the
'shrine'; the 'ritual grass'; 'transvestism'; the 'virgin's headdress'; the
'handing over ritual'; and the 'rending of the bag'. The first two I
classify as *persistent*, the second two as *developed* and the last two as
extinct for reasons which ought to become clear in the course of the
discussion.

3. Six Dominant Symbols

(i) Persistent

I have, I believe, demonstrated convincingly elsewhere that the
'shrine' or 'altar' of ritual plants known by the Nandi as *korosiot* is a
highly-condensed conventional symbol.[8] It is primarily religious,
thanksgiving and prayers to *Asis* and the ritual burning of plants being
central to its purpose. However, it is much else besides being a
religious symbol: it reinforces both social structure and economy.
Consider, for instance, the procession around it in strict ritual order of
social status and rank, the anointing by its side of clan and family
representatives and the smearing of cowdung at its base reflecting the
pastoral economy and 'sacredness' of cattle. Even today these ritual
actions are performed.

The latter-mentioned actions, reinforcing structure and economy,
may not be difficult to interpret either for the participant or the
observer; the aforementioned religious symbols and symbolic
behaviour, however, are understood by few. Indeed, the 'shrine' has
dropped out of use, being employed only on public occasions such as
initiation ceremonies and weddings. But in these rituals it has

persisted in a pervasive sense. The question is: 'Why has it persisted in public, although not in private?'

I was informed by a prominent leader of the Africa Inland Church and one of the earliest converts that when the first Christian preachers set foot in Aldai they were nicknamed by the Nandi *'Kipsomasis'*, literally, 'those who beg *Asis*'.[9] In other words, the Nandi thought of the Christian 'God' (English) or *'Mungu'* (Swahili) as equivalent to *Asis*, but found it rather difficult to comprehend the need to keep on begging him in prayer! Moreover, Catholic missionaries employed (and still do) a Nandi word for the deity, *Cheptalel* (literally, 'the shining one'). It is my guess therefore that the 'shrine' as a religious symbol was not considered at variance with the cosmology introduced by the changing order. Possibly the animal sacrifice associated with it was so considered and it has consequently disappeared. Confirming this suggestion on the one hand is the fact that no Nandi Christian ever mentioned the 'shrine' specifically as being inimical to Christian faith and on the other hand the fact that many did mention such acts as 'sacrifice', 'bathing in the nude', 'confession', 'oath-taking in secret' and the operation of circumcision or clitoridectomy itself as being un-Christian.

Elders, men and women alike, invoke *Asis*'s blessing at the 'shrine'. This may appear a necessary sanctioning of the younger generation by its elders and therefore justify the persistence of the 'shrine' and its attendant ceremony of spitting beer.

Thus, the employment of the 'shrine' pervades the rites. To omit the 'shrine' would mean displacing the focal point of much of the ritual. It would almost certainly mean denuding the ritual of all religious significance, a turning of ritual into 'mere ceremony'.[10]

These arguments should hold good for the persistence of the 'shrine' in the early years of change. But what of the latter years? For it has persisted right up to the present day. This cries out for explanation as so few Nandi today, young or old, have any idea of its overt religious significance. I suggest that what we have here is the opposite of what took place when the first Christians rejected certain aspects of the rituals. As the rites were curtailed and the 'shrine' went out of use as a domestic altar its significance for the Nandi traditional world view was forgotten. Culturally it stopped performing, or, to put it another way, at a conscious level it lost its powers of 'logico-meaningful' integration. Therefore, Catholic initiation elders and other Christians who hitherto had tried to purge the rites of 'pagan' elements turned a blind eye. But, we must hasten to add, the 'shrine' functions at another level, that of the unconscious. At this level, it conveys meaning in a 'mystical' sense through the employment of universal symbols such as the circle and the number four and of Nandi religious symbols relating to the sun. Were it not for this unconscious appeal and the reinforcement of social structure, the 'shrine' might well be emptied of its meaning and use today.

To sum up on the 'shrine' I should like to put a final question and attempt to answer it. But first to quote Clifford Geertz:

In most societies, where change is a characteristic rather than an abnormal occurrence, we shall expect to find more or less radical discontinuities between the two [the cultural and social aspects of human life]. I would argue that it is in these very discontinuities that we shall find some of the primary driving forces in change.[11]

How long can society contain the conflict between culture and social system? Only so long as the 'logico-meaningful' and the 'causal-functional' remain somewhat in step. When the time comes, the 'shrine', devoid of the power to develop or be transformed, will either become extinct or function only as an empty symbol. It will have failed to command confidence,[12] and will have become, like the pouring out of the first cup of spirits from an illicit still, a 'forgotten language'.[13]

Turning next to the question of the function and persistence of the 'ritual grass' — in Nandi *segutiet* — one is struck by parallels with the case of the 'shrine'. Before continuing, however, let me note the fact that although the 'ritual grass' is both dominant and conventional it is not such a highly-condensed symbol. Indeed, it is condensed only insofar as it is used (as a term) almost interchangeably with *katunisiet*, the word for marriage. Ordinarily used today the 'ritual grass' indicates the binding nature of marriage, although, strictly speaking, the marriage bond is not as unbreakable as in the past.

One reason, I suggest, for the persistence of the 'ritual grass' as a symbol is its resemblance, in nature and function, to the Christian 'ring'. This similarity has been pointed out to me more than once. A second is its endorsement by the Catholic Church (particularly Fr Kuhn) as a symbol of the once-for-all nature of marriage — even Nandi marriage — and therefore a custom which had to be respected.[14] Both these causes of persistence parallel those reasons suggested for the persistence of the 'shrine'.

It is interesting to speculate here how the Christian Church might have taken over the symbol of the 'ritual grass' and christianised it — transforming it in the process. But it is now too late. A young priest, presently in Nandi, suggested to his catechists and church leaders how he might introduce the knotty *nogirwet* stick and the 'ritual grass' into the Christian marriage ceremony (post-Vatican II).[15] But they were adamant in their desire to retain the Catholic ceremony in its entirety; it had become familiar to them and incidentally symbolic both of a particular (Christian) sub-culture and status accorded within it.

But also, I suggest, the 'ritual grass' persists as the symbol of Nandi marriage today because traditional marriage is still practised by a majority of Nandi people — Christians and traditionalists alike.

'Logico-meaningful' and 'causal-functional' integration are still to a great extent in step. It has been suggested by some — but at this point opinion differs — that, because of fear on behalf of parents that undesirable marriage will take place, the 'ritual grass' is tied at betrothal as well as at marriage. If this is so and, as Fr Kuhn emphasised, the 'ritual grass' is tending to become 'undone' for reasons not allowed traditionally, the discontinuities between culture and social system may become too great and the symbol's persistent position jeopardised.

To sum up on the subject of *persistence*. We can confidently affirm that when, in a time of social change, culture and social system keep in step, certain dominant symbols persist. Moreover, their persistence must be attributed in large measure to the effective control of elders who hold the secrets and possess the skills of ritual procedure: it is they who as custodians of traditional values pass on the themes of a culture. But although dominant symbols may persist, if and when these symbols are highly-condensed, they also suffer the loss of component parts and a diminution in their powers of communication.[16] Likewise, although a symbol may persist, its meaning may change.

(ii) *Developed*

The persistence and development (with a certain amount of transformation) of *transvestism* in the female initiation rite as against its virtual disappearance in the male equivalent is one of the most interesting and intriguing of all aspects relating to the effects of change on Nandi ritual. To the best of my knowledge, whatever its purpose, it involved in the past the transvestism of the girl only in simple warrior attire: there was no elaboration. But today, the dress is not only extremely elaborate but a highly-condensed symbol. Why single out this symbol for development (and in the process rob it of some of its original meaning as a symbol of rebellion)? I have several suggestions to make — all, I believe, quite probable answers.

First, and most important, the initiative in this ritual act was and still is held to a great extent by the younger generation. Traditionally it was, and nowadays it is, the prerogative of the initiand's 'sweetheart' to dress her. It is clear from looking at the ritual today that the dress itself and the events surrounding the transvestism — pop music, modern dance, the serving of soft drinks and sweets — are orientated to the young person's scene. I have already described both the ritual and the dress, suffice it to mention further the importance of bringing together the modern symbols of young Nandi manhood — the school tie, the shirt, the plimsolls — with the old — the headdress, the 'kilt', the leglets of colobus monkey skin and the thigh-bells.

Granting that the symbol was developed largely by youth I can go one step further and assert that it affirms the values of youth:

education, athletics, Nandi-consciousness and nation-consciousness. But, most important, it affirms that virtue which bridges the generation gap and features high in Nandi social values — bravery. Bravery figures large like a floodlit bridge across the generations and is cited as the most important lesson learnt at initiation. In transvestism it assumes mythical proportions.

I can make a further suggestion by adding that development in the elaboration of the dress gives scope to the newly-acquired skills of the female sex gained in the needlework classes of mission, school and women's guild.

So viewed, transvestism is a good example of a highly-condensed symbol, remarkably adapted to change and exhibiting a very high degree of correlation between cultural and social systems. I judge it extremely successful in the degree of integration achieved and for this a great deal of credit goes to the imagination of youth. When I attended the ritual performance at Sang'alo I found that the schoolboy brother of the initiand obviously took a great pride in her looks. So too, I noticed that numerous informants described with great detail and pride costumes made or hired for such occasions.

I like to think that I have observed, in the working of this single exciting symbol, a demonstration (in Durkheim's terms) of 'how a symbol may succeed in concentrating upon itself all the power that properly belongs only to the ultimate reality it represents.'[17]

The 'virgin's headdress' in Nandi exhibits quite a different type of development. It is the only successful attempt (so far as I know) by any section of the Christian Church to take over a traditional Nandi symbol and transform it for use in a Christian context. Indeed, mention of it reminds me of how one Sunday morning, as I watched a Nandi Orthodox priest administer baptism and chrismation, I was struck by the similarity of his ritual actions to Nandi 'hair-cutting', 'anointing' and 'immersion'. They cried out for interpretation in terms of Nandi culture.

I was introduced to the concept of the modern 'virgin's headdress' — *sianya* in Nandi — by an Anglican vicar's wife belonging to the East African Revival Movement and living at Kebulonik in North Nandi.[18] She explained how Christian parents despaired of keeping their daughters from becoming pregnant before marriage and devised the *sianya*, a Christian version of the traditional 'virgin's headdress', known in Nandi as *nariet*.[19] It was embroidered and sewn by a Christian neighbour, white nylon ribbon being sewn to look like the traditional tusks, and worn by a young virgin bride on her wedding day. Dorcas's own daughter had the honour of wearing it and being given eight cattle in recognition of her virginity.

An interesting aspect of the development of this symbol is that the initiative is being taken by the Christians when traditional and Christian values coincide and in an area where there is conflict at present between culture and social system. Moreover, following on this initiative in introducing the modern 'virgin's headdress' came the invitation by local women, Christian and non-Christian alike, for Dorcas to give them instruction on how to help their daughters retain their virginity; this in the face of being accused by their menfolk of not fulfilling their role of giving the girls satisfactory training.

To sum up, I find in the modern 'virgin's headdress' an interesting attempt to influence social behaviour by appealing to the deterrent and didactic powers potentially present in a time-honoured traditional symbol transferred to a modern setting. There is no means as yet by which to judge the ultimate success of the attempt.

(iii) *Extinct*

A very obvious extinct symbol to select for analysis is the 'handing over' ceremony at which a white bullock used to be slaughtered. All that the slaughter of a bullock before a ritual indicates nowadays is that the host is wealthy and expects many guests.

Events leading to the abandonment of the ritual slaughter took place in stages and have been recounted in detail elsewhere.[20] Particularly important was the ban imposed by the colonial government.

The abandonment is a good example of how a symbol disappears through enforced disuse and fails to be relevant when opportunity comes for revival. The evidence, moreover, indicates how the disappearance of the appropriate ritual beginning and ending the different age-set periods of office has contributed to the loss of age-set identity and solidarity.

We might compare here parallel enforcement of action among the Terik and Kikuyu but with respect to female circumcision. It will be recalled how a Luyia chief introduced sanctions against the circumcision of girls in Terik and his action led to the virtual disappearance of the rite so much so that some ethnographers do not report the existence of the custom at all. In Kikuyu a survey conducted among secondary schoolgirls in 1972 revealed that on average 68 per cent Catholics were circumcised, 37 per cent Anglicans and only 7 per cent Presbyterians. It was the Church of Scotland Mission's requirement that its members and employees sign a pledge renouncing female circumcision which precipitated the crisis of 1929 in Kikuyuland. But whatever the intervening years brought it cannot be denied that these efforts were successful in the primary objective of eliminating the ritual.[21]

In conclusion, therefore, what remains to be seen is whether the prohibition of a symbol by external forces makes its re-introduction at a later stage either extremely unlikely or simply difficult. It could be that major adjustments and changes in interpretation would make re-introduction possible although difficult.

Similarly, external forces were involved in the disappearance of the 'rending of the bag' — in Nandi *kebet lol* — but not in the same legislative manner. Today it is very rare to find anybody in Nandi who has actually witnessed the ritual of 'rending the bag'. Admittedly it was performed on rare occasions even in the past but an explanation is ready to hand.

It will be recalled that in the Tindiret area, bordering on Kipsigis country, the 'anointing' ritual practised among the Kipsigis, for the purposes of recognising divorce, has been introduced into Nandi. It not only recognises divorce but permits it to a couple with children. Other Nandi go to the courts and yet others give the hurricane lamp to the female partner.

Reasons for this are obvious. First, the denial by missionary and administrator of the Nandi ideal of life-long marriage was demonstrated in the seeking of divorce for Christian converts and the re-marriage of divorcees and widows. Secondly, the Nandi acceptance of things as they are, their pragmatic, realistic, approach, led to the adjustment of culture to social system and the adaptation of ritual to practice. What 'rending the bag' symbolised was no longer held either in theory or in practice and so the symbol was abandoned in favour of another.

To sum up, the discontinuities between culture and social system had become so strong as to force change. The change brought the 'logico-meaningful' and the 'causal-functional' once more into step and a measure of integration was reintroduced into Nandi life.

4. *Authority Structure and Change*

When the reader reflects on the foregoing it becomes immediately obvious how important a part change in the structures of authority plays in ritual change.

Let us together take the six dominant symbols one by one in order to make the point:

(i) *Persistent*

It was within the elders' control to retain the 'shrine' as a symbol; this they did and so ensured its survival and ultimate persistence. So too with the 'ritual grass': it remained within the province of the ritual specialists and tribal elders.

(ii) *Developed*

When we turn to *transvestism*, however, we are on quite different ground. Authority in this particular matter has shifted — to the educated youth and to some extent to the educational authorities who determine the length and something of the character of the modern initiation rite. As for the modern 'virgin's headdress' it only becomes explicable at all through the erosion of the women elders' authority and the development of a new centre of authority in the pastor's wife.

(iii) *Extinct*

As for the 'handing over' ceremony it was forced out of existence by the imposition of another authority over and above that of the tribal. In quite a different manner but with the same consequences 'rending the bag' was replaced by a different kind of divorce ritual: the ideal of life-long marriage had become eroded so that 'rending the bag' failed to satisfy the requirements of society.

5. *Dynamics of Change*

The six symbols selected for analysis and classification as *persistent, developed* and *extinct* are but a few of the many which may be noted by a re-reading of the ritual descriptions. The exercise has been useful in enabling us to discover principles which ought to be applicable in the wider context of ritual and social change everywhere. Diagramatically, the principles could be represented as follows:

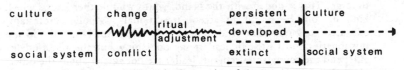

Figure 4. Dynamics of change

In drawing this study to a close — a study which has enabled us to see ritual change in its historical context — I should like to choose a statement of Monica Wilson's for comment:

What particular symbols are retained, or borrowed, or transformed depends upon what catches the imagination. A poet's associations always lie within the frame of his experience as a member of a particular society with a given culture, but inside that frame his imagination roves; the symbols used in rituals are poetic or dramatic forms accepted by a community through time.[22]

I think that I have shown that, for the Nandi at least, the *persistence, development* or *extinction* of certain symbols is by no means arbitrary, can occur in a relatively short time and depends not only upon what catches the imagination but upon much else besides. Symbols used in ritual are much more than poetic or dramatic forms: they may be said even to participate somehow in the reality they are intended to signify. Symbolic change is in fact determined by a variety of factors: some without, others within society's control. Society shapes ritual but ritual continues to affect society. And it does so when it pursues, consciously or unconsciously, adjustments between culture and social system, between the ordered system of meaning and symbols and the pattern of social interaction itself. Such adjustments contribute to the maintenance of a people's equilibrium. Thus ritual is seen, not only to exist in but to act as a stabilising factor in a rapidly changing society.

NOTES

1 Monica Wilson, *Religion and the Transformation of Society*, Cambridge, 1971, p. 130.
2 See my 'Ritual Change among the Nandi', ch. II: 'The Nandi'.
3 Ibid., ch. III: 'The Nandi and Christian Missions'.
4 A Nandi young person's lack of identity is not the same as that discussed by Monica Wilson in *Religion and the Transformation of Society*, pp. 144-5. She refers to the difficulty 'experienced by individuals in accepting their roots when they live through a period of radical change' as familiar in the case of immigrants to the United States and analysed by Professor Erik Erikson in his *Insight and Responsibility*, New York, 1964. The immigrant has his roots to accept, to maintain personal integrity, but once he has done that he has a new recognisable identity to forge. This is not so with the Nandi youth who neither knows which kind of root he ought to accept (traditional, Catholic, Protestant, educated etc.) nor what kind of society to adapt to. Not only do the missionaries and Christian leaders say one thing but the traditionalist elder and the young intellectualist leader are not agreed about the other.
5 Mary Douglas, *Natural Symbols*, pp. 83-4.
6 Note Mary Douglas' further discussion, particularly concerning 'sacralised institutions', ibid., pp. 87-91.
7 Cf. Clifford Geertz, 'Ritual and Social Change: A Javanese Example' in *American Anthropologist*, Vol. LXI, 1959, reprinted in his *The Interpretation of Cultures: Selected Essays*, New York/London, 1975, pp. 142-69.
8 See the Appendix ''*Koros*' in my 'Ritual Change among the Nandi', pp. 342-54.
9 Jeremiah Arap Birir, in an interview in Kapsabet, July 1974; he has now committed some of his interview material to writing in the form of a mimeographed paper of the history of the AIC in Nandi.
10 J.S. La Fontaine, 'Ritualization of Women's Life-Crises in Bugisu' in J.S. La Fontaine (ed.), *The Interpretation of Ritual*, pp. 159-86. She relates how some rituals disappeared, becoming what she calls 'ceremonials' and how marriage became more elaborate, absorbing elements from the Christian wedding and thus remaining 'ritual'. Cf. Monica Wilson, 'The Wedding Cakes: A Study of Social Change', in J.S. La Fontaine (ed.), op. cit., pp. 187-201.
11 Clifford Geertz, loc. cit., p. 144.

12 Mary Douglas, *Purity and Danger*, Harmondsworth, 1970, p. 86: 'In comparing magic with false currency Mauss was wrong. Money can only perform its role of intensifying economic interaction if the public has faith in it. If faith in it is shaken, the currency is useless. So too with ritual; its symbols can only have effect so long as they command confidence.'

13 Watching the Irishman pour the contents of the cup on the ground, Seán Ó'Faoláin asked: 'Why do you empty that cup?' and received the reply, 'I dunno, we always do it.' (Quoted from *The Listener* by Monica Wilson in *Religion and the Transformation of Society*, p. 72.)

14 The different attitudes of Catholics and Protestants to the traditional culture were very evident in Nandi. The relevant example here is that missionaries of the Africa Inland Mission did not consider Nandi marriage 'marriage in the eyes of God'.

15 Personal communication from Martin Boyle at Chepterit.

16 It is possible, but I do not think likely, that this gives some support to Audrey Richards' and I. Schapera's hypothesis that 'magic rites tend to survive in contact with Europeanism while religious ceremonies associated with moral values or prayers to ancestral spirits tend to be abandoned.' I am thinking of course of the 'mystical' or 'magical' aspects of the *korosiot* shrine; otherwise there is no direct parallel in Nandi. Cf. *Chisungu*, p. 139.

17 The words are Firth's summary of Durkheim's position. See *Symbols*, p. 132.

18 Dorcas Chebunde Tapkere, wife of Abraham Saina, at Kebulonik in December 1973.

19 From *siang'anet*, the strap used for attaching a bell to a cow's neck; both traditionally and according to the Christian practice the 'tusks' are attached to one of these straps and a bell dangles behind the girl's back.

20 See my 'Ritual Change among the Nandi', pp. 114-18.

21 Personal communication from Jocelyn Murray, and in her paper, 'The Present Status of "Female Circumcision" among Kikuyu and Embu Secondary Schoolgirls, with Reference to the Historical Background', University of California, Los Angeles, 1972. Granted, no attention is paid to change of affiliation or choice of allegiance to a particular group.

22 Monica Wilson in 'The Wedding Cakes: A Study of Ritual Change', loc. cit., p. 200.

Select Bibliography
and Written Sources

1. Abbreviations

AR   Annual Report

CROMIA   'Churches' Research Project on Marriage in Africa', numbered consecutively, e.g., CROMIA/1, CROMIA/2 etc. Set up on 16 March 1970. Fr Aylward Shorter, WF, was the Organising Secretary.

DC/NDI/1/1, etc. District Commissioner/Nandi/File No.

NDPR   Nandi District Political Records, Kenya National Archives, Nairobi.

NDR   Nandi District Records, Kenya National Archives, Nairobi.

QR   Quarterly Report

2. Mission Publications and Records

'Africa Inland Church Constitution with Rules and Regulations' (mimeographed), n.d.

'Memorandum Prepared by the Kikuyu Mission Council on Female Circumcision' (mimeographed), Kikuyu, Church of Scotland Mission, 1931.

Church Missionary Gleaner, 1910.

Church Missionary Intelligencer, 1906.

Church Missionary Society Report, 1910-11; 1912-13.

Mission (organ of the Bible Churchmen's Missionary Society), Vol. VII, No. 2, March/April 1970.

The Missionary Messenger (organ of the Bible Churchmen's Missionary Society), Vol. XXXV, No. 4, July/August 1957; Vol. XXXV, No. 6, November/December 1957; Vol. XXXIX, No. 1, January/February 1961; Vol. XLI, No. 5, September/October 1963.

Africa Inland Church Records at Kapsabet.

Anglican Church Records at Kapsabet.

Catholic Mission Records at Chepterit and Tindinyo.

Full Gospel Church Records at Nandi Hills.

International Pentecostal Assemblies Records at Chepkumia.

Pentecostal Assemblies of Canada Records at Nyang'ori.

Seventh-day Adventist Church Records at Kaigat.

3. Government Publications and Records

Handbook of Kenya Colony and Protectorate (1920), Naval Staff Intelligence Division (material collected during the Great War).

Historical Survey of the Origins and Growth of Mau Mau (1960), F.D. Corfield, Nairobi, Government Printer.

Kenya: An Official Handbook (1973) published by the East African Publishing House for the Government of the Republic of Kenya.

Kenya Population Census, 1969 (Vol. I, 1970; Vols II, III, 1971), Nairobi, Statistics Division, Ministry of Finance and Economic Planning.

Laws of Kenya (1962), revised ed., chs CL-CLVII:
  CL *The Marriage Ordinance*
  CLI *The African Christian Marriage and Divorce Ordinance*
  CLII *The Matrimonial Causes Ordinance*
  CLIII *The Subordinate Courts (Separation and Maintenance) Ordinance*
  CLIV *The Maintenance Orders Enforcement Ordinance*
  CLV *The Mohammedan Marriage and Divorce Registration Ordinance*
  CLVI *The Mohammedan Marriage, Divorce and Succession Ordinance*
  CLVII *The Hindu Marriage and Divorce Ordinance*
  Nairobi, the Government Printer.
Nandi Work and Culture (1950) (mimeographed) prepared by G.W.B. Huntingford, Colonial Research Studies, No. 4, London, H.M.S.O.
Report of the Commission on the Law of Marriage and Divorce (1968) Nairobi, the Government Printer. (Eugene Cotran, Member and Secretary.)
Court, Hospital and Marriage Records at Kapsabet Government offices.
Marriage Records at the office of the Registrar General, Nairobi.

4. *Unpublished Sources*

Ehret, Christopher (1974) 'Some Possible Trends in Precolonial Religious Thought in Kenya and Tanzania', paper read at the Conference on the Historical Study of African Religions, Nairobi, June 1974.
Gold, Alice (1974a) 'A Pre-colonial Economic History of the Nandi', a paper in African History, University of California, Los Angeles.
_____ (1974b) 'The Economic Role of the Nandi Woman in the 19th and 20th Centuries', prepared for the University of California, Los Angeles, African Studies Centre Colloquium 'Women and Change in Africa: 1870-1970'.
Kerich, N.K. (1972) 'The Nandi Religious System', a paper in Religious Studies, University of Nairobi.
Kipkorir, Benjamin E. (1974) 'The Sun in Marakwet Religious Thought', paper read at the Conference on the Historical Study of African Religions, Nairobi, June 1974.
Langley, Myrtle S. (1976) 'Ritual Change among the Nandi: A Study of Change in Life-Crisis Rituals 1923-1973', Ph.D. thesis, U. of Bristol.
Merritt, Hilton (1970) 'Traditional Circumcision in Tiriki', research paper.
Murray, Jocelyn (1972) 'The Present Status of "Female Circumcision" among Kikuyu and Embu Secondary Schoolgirls, with Reference to the Historical Background', University of California, Los Angeles, research paper.
_____ (1974) 'The Kikuyu Female Circumcision Controversy of 1928-31: Background, Comparisons and Perspectives', doctoral dissertation, University of California, Los Angeles.
Mwanzi, H.A. (1974) 'Nilo-Bantu Interaction in Western Kenya: A Case Study of the Evolution of Religious Concepts of the Kipsigis', paper read at the Conference on the Historical Study of African Religions, Nairobi, June 1974.
Shorter, Aylward (1972) 'Notes on Traditional and Christian Marriage in Africa', CROMIA/11, Gaba, Kampala, Pastoral Institute of Eastern Africa.
Too, Henry (1973) 'A History of the Nandi Laibons', private paper.

5. *Published Sources*

Barton, C. and Juxon, T. (1923) 'Notes on the Kipsigis or Lumbwa Tribe of Kenya Colony' in *Journal of the Royal Anthropological Institute*, Vol. LIII, 1923.

Bernardi, B. (1952) 'The Age-System of the Nilo-Hamitic Peoples' in *Africa*, Vol. XXII, 1952.

Bettelheim, Bruno (1955) *Symbolic Wounds: Puberty Rites and the Envious Male*, London, Thames & Hudson; Glencoe, Ill., Free Press (1954).

Bryson, Stuart M. (1959) *Light in Darkness: The Story of the Nandi Bible*, London, Parry Jackman.

Cherotich, Sarah (1967) 'The Nandi Female Initiation and Marriage and Christian Impact upon It' in *Dini na Mila*, Vol. II, No. 2/3, Kampala, 1967.

Cotran, Eugene (1968) *Restatement of African Law: Kenya I: Marriage and Divorce*, London, Sweet & Maxwell.

Dale, Ivan R. and Greenway, P.J. (1961) *Kenya Trees and Shrubs*, Nairobi, Buchanan's Kenya Estates Ltd., in association with Hatchards, London.

Douglas, Mary (1970) *Purity and Danger*, Harmondsworth, Penguin Books.

———— (1973) *Natural Symbols*, Harmondsworth, Penguin Books.

Durkheim, Émile (1915) *The Elementary Forms of the Religious Life*, London, George Allen and Unwin.

Ehret, Christopher (1968) 'Linguistics as a Tool for Historians' in B.A. Ogot (ed.) *Hadith 1*, Nairobi, East African Publishing House.

———— (1971) *Southern Nilotic History: Linguistic Approaches to the Study of the Past*, Evanston, Ill., Northwestern University Press.

———— (1973) 'Cushites and the Highland and Plains Nilotes' in B.A. Ogot (ed.) *Zamani: A Survey of East African History* (New Edition), Nairobi, East African Publishing House.

Eliot, Sir Charles (1905) *The East Africa Protectorate*, London, Edward Arnold. Reprinted 1966, New York, Barnes and Noble.

Evans-Pritchard, E.E. (1940) 'The Political Structure of the Nandi-Speaking Peoples of Kenya' in *Africa*, Vol. XIII, 1940.

———— (1951) *Kinship and Marriage among the Nuer*, Oxford, Clarendon Press.

———— (1965) 'Some Collective Expressions of Obscenity in Africa' in his *The Position of Women in Primitive Societies and Other Essays in Social Anthropology*, London, Faber & Faber, pp. 76-101.

Erikson, Erik (1964) *Insight and Responsibility*, New York, Norton.

Farrant Russell, S. (1972) *Full Fifty Years: The BCMS Story*, London, Patmos Press.

Firth, Sir Raymond (1973) *Symbols: Public and Private*, London, George Allen & Unwin.

Foley, W.M. (1915) 'Christian Marriage' in James Hastings (ed.) *The Encyclopaedia of Religion and Ethics*, Vol. VIII, Edinburgh, T. & T. Clark.

Fortes, Meyer (1962) 'Ritual and Office' in M. Gluckman (ed.) *Essays on the Ritual of Social Relations*, Manchester University Press.

Geertz, Clifford (1957) 'Ethos, World View and the Analysis of Sacred Symbols' in *The Antioch Review*, Vol. XVII, No. 4, 1957.

———— (1959) 'Ritual and Social Change: A Javanese Example' in *American Anthropologist*, Vol. LXI, 1959.

_____ (1964) 'Ideology as a Cultural System' in D. Apter (ed.) *Ideology and Discontent*, Glencoe, Ill., The Free Press.

_____ (1966) 'Religion as a Cultural System' in M. Banton (ed.) *Anthropological Approaches to the Study of Religion*, London, Tavistock.

_____ (1973) 'Thick Description: Toward an Interpretative Theory of Culture' in Clifford Geertz, *The Interpretation of Cultures: Selected Essays*, New York, Basic Books; London, Hutchinson, 1975. The collection includes all those mentioned above.

Van Gennep, Arnold (1960) *The Rites of Passage*, Chicago, at the University Press; London, Routledge. First published as *Les rites de passage*, 1908, and transl. from French by Monika B. Vizedom and Gabrielle L. Caffee.

Gluckman, Max (1954) *Rituals of Rebellion in South-East Africa*, Manchester University Press.

_____ (1956) *Custom and Conflict in Africa*, Oxford, Basil Blackwell.

_____ (ed.) (1962) *Essays on the Ritual of Social Relations*, Manchester University Press.

_____ (1963) *Order and Rebellion in Tribal Africa*, London, Cohen and West.

_____ (1965) *Politics, Law and Ritual in Tribal Society*, Oxford, Basil Blackwell.

Goldschmidt, W. (1967) *Sebei Law*, Berkeley and Los Angeles, University of California Press.

Goody, Jack (1961) 'Religion and Ritual: The Definitional Problem' in *The British Journal of Sociology*, Vol. XII, June 1961.

Greenstein, Lewis (1975) 'Africans in a European War: The First World War in East Africa with Special Reference to the Nandi of Kenya', doctoral dissertation, University of Indiana. Reproduced by University Microfilms International, Ann Arbor, Michigan, 1978.

Hartley, Eugene L. (1964) 'Symbolism' in J. Gould and W.W. Kolb (eds) *A Dictionary of the Social Sciences*, London, Tavistock.

Hastings, Adrian (1973) *Christian Marriage in Africa* (Being a Report commissioned by the Archbishops of Cape Town, Central Africa, Kenya, Tanzania and Uganda), London, SPCK.

Herbert, J.S. (1910-11) Report on Nandi in the *Church Missionary Society Report, 1910-11*, pp. 475-6, London, Church Missionary Society.

Hobley, C.W. (1902) *Eastern Uganda: An Ethnological Survey*, London, Anthropological Institute of Great Britain and Ireland.

Hollis, A.C. (1909) *The Nandi. Their Language and Folklore* Oxford, Clarendon Press.

Huntingford, G.W.B. (1944) *The Nandi*, Nairobi, Peoples of Kenya Series, No. 11.

_____ (1953a) *The Nandi of Kenya: Tribal Control in a Pastoral Society*, London, Routledge.

_____ (1953b) *The Northern Nilo-Hamites*, London, International African Institute, for the Ethnographic Survey of Africa.

_____ (1953c) *The Southern Nilo-Hamites*, London, International African Institute, for the Ethnographic Survey of Africa.

_____ (1963) 'The Peopling of the Interior of East Africa by its Modern Inhabitants' in R. Oliver and G. Mathew (eds) *History of East Africa*, Vol. I, Oxford, Clarendon Press.

———— (1963) 'Nandi Witchcraft' in John Middleton and E.H. Winter (eds) *Witchcraft and Sorcery in East Africa*, London, Routledge.

Jackson, Sir Frederick (1930) *Early Days in East Africa*, London, Edw. Arnold.

Jaffé, Aniela (1964) 'Symbols and the Visual Arts' in C.G. Jung, *Man and His Symbols*, London, Aldus Books.

Johnston, Sir H.H. (1902) *The Uganda Protectorate*, 2 vols., London, Hutchinson.

Jung, Carl G. (1964) *Man and His Symbols*, London, Aldus Books.

King, Noel Q. (1970) *Religions of Africa*, New York, Harper and Row.

Kipkorir, B.E. with Welbourn, F.B. (1973) *The Marakwet of Kenya: A Preliminary Study*, Nairobi, East African Literature Bureau.

Kisembo, Benezeri; Magesa, Laurenti and Shorter, Aylward (1977) *African Christian Marriage*, London, Geoffrey Chapman.

La Fontaine, J.S. (ed.) (1972) *The Interpretation of Ritual: Essays in Honour of A.I. Richards*, London, Tavistock (her own contribution entitled 'Ritualization of Women's Life-Crises in Bugisu').

Le Vine, Robert A. and Sangree, Walter H. (1962) 'The Diffusion of Age-Group Organization in East Africa: A Controlled Comparison' in *Africa*, Vol. XXXII, No. 2, April 1962.

Lang'at, S.C. (1969) 'Some Aspects of Kipsigis History before 1914' in B.G. McIntosh (ed.) *Ngano*, Nairobi, East African Publishing House.

Langley, Myrtle S. and Kiggins, Tom (1974) *A Serving People: A Textbook on the Church in East Africa*, Nairobi, Oxford University Press.

Macpherson, R. (1970) *The Presbyterian Church in Kenya*, Nairobi, Presbyterian Church of East Africa.,

McKemey, Robert (1963) 'The Church in Nandi' in *The Missionary Messenger*, Vol. XLI, No. 5, Sept./Oct. 1963, London, Bible Churchmen's Missionary Society.

Magut, P.K. Arap (1969) 'The Rise and Fall of the Nandi Orkoiyot c. 1850-1957' in B.G. McIntosh (ed.) *Ngano*, Nairobi, East African Publishing House.

Mair, Lucy (1953) 'African Marriage and Social Change' in Arthur Phillips (ed.) *Survey of African Marriage and Family Life*, London, Oxford University Press, for the International African Institute; reprinted by Cass, 1969, as *African Marriage and Social Change*.

Manners, Robert A. (1967) 'The Kipsigis of Kenya' in Julian H. Steward (ed.) *Contemporary Change in Traditional Societies, Vol. I: Introduction and African Tribes*, Illinois, at the University Press.

Massam, J.A. (1927) *The Cliff Dwellers of Kenya*, London, Seeley; reprinted by Cass, 1968.

Matson, A.T. (1970) 'Nandi Traditions on Raiding' in B.A. Ogot (ed.) *Hadith 2*, Nairobi, East African Publishing House.

———— (1972a) 'Reflections on the Growth of Political Consciousness in Nandi' in B.A. Ogot (ed.) *Hadith 4: Politics and Nationalism in Colonial Kenya*, Nairobi, East African Publishing House.

———— (1972b) *Nandi Resistance to British Rule 1890-1906*, Nairobi, East African Publishing House.

———— (1974) *The Nandi Campaign against the British 1895-1906*, Transafrica Historical Papers, No. 1, Nairobi, Transafrica Publishers.

Meinertzhagen, R. (1957) *Kenya Diary: 1902-6*, Edinburgh, Oliver & Boyd.

Mumford, Frances J. (1959) *Nandi Studies: A Textbook of Nandi Grammar and Idiom*, Kapsabet, Africa Inland Mission.

Ng'eny, Samuel K. Arap (1970) 'Nandi Resistance to the Establishment of British Administration 1883-1906' in B.A. Ogot (ed.) *Hadith 2*, Nairobi, East African Publishing House.

Orchardson, Ian Q. (1961) *The Kipsigis* (abridged, edited and partly rewritten by A.T. Matson from original MS, 1929-37, Kericho), Nairobi, East African Publishing House.

Orde Browne, G. St John (1925) *The Vanishing Tribes of Kenya*, London, Seeley.

Peristiany, J.G. (1939) *The Social Institutions of the Kipsigis*, London, Routledge.

Phillips, Arthur (1953) 'An Introductory Essay' in Arthur Phillips (ed.) *Survey of African Marriage and Family Life*, London, Oxford University Press; reprinted in Arthur Phillips and Henry F. Morris, *Marriage Laws in Africa*, London, Oxford University Press, for the International African Institute.

Radcliffe-Brown, A.R. and Forde, Daryll (1950) *African Systems of Kinship and Marriage*, London, Oxford University Press, for International African Institute.

Ravenhill, Philip L. (1978) 'The Interpretation of Symbolism in Wan Female Initiation' in *Africa*, Vol. XLVIII, No. 1, 1978.

Richards, Audrey I. (1956) *Chisungu: A Girls' Initiation Ceremony among the Bemba of Northern Rhodesia*, London, Faber and Faber.

Richardson, Kenneth (1968) *Garden of Miracles: A History of the Africa Inland Mission*, London, Victory Press.

Ruel, M.J. (1962) 'Kuria Generation Classes' in *Africa*, Vol. XXXII, 1962.

Salvadori, Cynthia and Fedders, Andrew (1973) *Maasai*, London, Collins.

Sangree, Walter H. (1966) *Age, Prayer and Politics in Tiriki, Kenya*, London, Oxford University Press, for the East African Institute of Social Research.

Sapir, Edward (1934) 'Symbolism' in *Encyclopaedia of the Social Sciences*, Vol. XIV, New York, Macmillan; reprinted in David G. Mandelbaum (ed.) *Selected Writings of Edward Sapir*, Berkeley, University of California Press.

Shorter, Aylward (1973) *African Culture and the Christian Church: An Introduction to Social and Pastoral Anthropology*, London, Geoffrey Chapman.

———— (1974) *East African Societies*, London, Routledge.

Snell, G.S. (1954) *Nandi Customary Law*, London, Macmillan.

Southall, Aidan W. (1972) 'Twinship and Symbolic Structure' in J.S. La Fontaine (ed.) *The Interpretation of Ritual*, London, Tavistock.

Spencer, Paul (1970) 'The Function of Ritual in the Socialization of the Samburu Moran' in Philip Mayer (ed.) *Socialization: The Approach from Social Anthropology*, London, Tavistock.

Sperber, Dan (1975) *Rethinking Symbolism*, Cambridge University Press.

Sutton, J.E.G. (1970) 'Some Reflections on the Early History of Western Kenya' in B.A. Ogot (ed.) *Hadith 2*, Nairobi, East African Publishing House.

———— (1973a) 'The Settlement of East Africa' in B.A. Ogot (ed.) *Zamani: A Survey of East African History*, new edn, Nairobi, East African Publishing House/Longman.

_____ (1973b) *The Archaeology of the Western Highlands of Kenya*, Memoir No. 3 of the British Institute in Eastern Africa, Nairobi, British Institute in Eastern Africa.

Swantz, Marja-Liisa (1970) *Ritual and Symbol in Transitional Zaramo Society*, Lund, Gleerup.

Syson, W.S. (1910) Report on the Progress of the Nandi Mission in the *Church Missionary Gleaner*, 1910, London, Church Missionary Society.

Turner, Victor W. (1962) 'Three Symbols of *Passage* in Ndembu Circumcision Ritual: *An Interpretation*' in Max Gluckman (ed.) *Essays on the Ritual of Social Relations*, Manchester University Press.

_____ (1966) 'Colour Classification in Ndembu Ritual' in M. Banton (ed.) *Anthropological Approaches to the Study of Religion*, London, Tavistock.

_____ (1967) 'Symbols in Ndembu Ritual' in his *The Forest of Symbols*, Ithaca (New York), Cornell University Press.

_____ (1968) *The Drums of Affliction*, Oxford, Clarendon Press, for International African Institute.

_____ (1969a) *The Ritual Process: Structure and Anti-Structure*, London, Routledge; Chicago, Aldine.

_____ (1969b) 'Symbolization and Patterning in the Circumcision Rites of Two Bantu-Speaking Societies' in M. Douglas and P.M. Kaberry (eds) *Man in Africa*, London, Tavistock.

_____ (1972) 'Symbols in African Ritual' in *Science*, Vol. CLXXIX, March 1972, pp. 1100-5; reprinted in J.L. Dolgin, D.S. Kemnitzer, and D.M. Schneider (eds) *Symbolic Anthropology: A Reader in the Study of Symbols and Meanings*, New York, Columbia University Press, 1977.

Welbourn, F.B. (1968) 'Keyo Initiation' in *Journal of Religion in Africa*, Vol. I, 1968.

Willis, J.J. (1906) 'The Mission of the Uganda Church' in the *Church Missionary Gleaner*, 1910, London, Church Missionary Society.

Willis, Roy (ed.) (1975) *The Interpretation of Symbolism*, ASA Studies 3, London, Malaby.

Wilson, Monica (1954) 'Nyakyusa Ritual and Symbolism' in *American Anthropologist*, Vol. LVI, No. 2, Part I, April 1954.

_____ (1957) *Rituals of Kinship among the Nyakyusa*, London, Oxford University Press, for International African Institute.

_____ (1959) *Communal Rituals of the Nyakyusa*, London, Oxford University Press, for International Institute.

_____ (1971) *Religion and the Transformation of Society*, Cambridge University Press.

Index and Glossary

In the case of Nandi words and phrases, with the exception of quotations from other writers, the orthography is that employed in the Kalenjin Bible, 1969.

145